WINERIES OF THE WORLD

WINERIES OF THE WORLD
Architecture and Viniculture

Oscar Riera Ojeda & Victor Deupi

New York · Paris · London · Milan

TABLE OF CONTENTS

INTRODUCTION / VICTOR DEUPI	8
VINEYARDS	16
ARCHITECTS' PROFILES	264
AUTHORS' PROFILES	269
BOOK CREDITS	272

Introduction
Victor Deupi

O Lord of the Naiads and of the Bacchanals who have the strength to uproot tall ash trees with their bare hands, nothing small or in a low style, nothing mortal, shall I sing. It is an intoxicating danger, o God of the wine press, to follow your divinity, wreathing my temples with green vine leaves. (Horace, Odes III:25)

There are few building types today that are so universally cherished and loved like the modern winery. Typically found throughout the world where pastoral arcadian landscapes allow for the cultivation of grapes or vine-growing, there are as many differences in the premises that accommodate the simple art of winemaking as there are in the regional, climatic, and topographical conditions that encourage the planting of vineyards. Although winemaking can take place in a variety of building types and locations, the structures that house such processing facilities require greater sophistication today, as they must respond more efficiently to energy and resource consumption, material lifespan and green building practices, suit the particular winemaking processes of the estate, and provide a compelling image that is universally recognized as part of the ever-expanding tourist and consumer market for wine.

Architecture and wine have been intimately connected since the very earliest societies serendipitously discovered that the fermentation of grapes was in fact a gift of the gods. So fortunate was this divine revelation that cautionary tales had to be established in order to curb the potentially damaging consequences of the magical elixir. And so, the myths of the young and handsome Bacchus (Dionysus in Greek), trained by his grotesque companion and tutor, the drunken Silenus, emerged to remind people that unless one curtails the appetites, there is little room for redemption. As such, few major temples were erected to the worship of the ancient gods of viniculture and pleasure as there have been both positive and negative attitudes towards the consumption of wine from ancient writers on agriculture and medicine from the start. Apart from the colossal Corinthian Temple of Bacchus at Baalbek, Lebanon, and the Temple of Silenus at Elis in the Peloponnese, only smaller sanctuaries and shrines were typically associated with such conspicuous Dionysian rituals. There was also no official Roman feast dedicated to the god of wine, though the Roman Senate suppressed in 186 BCE the bacchanalia (an organized festival of drunkenness and sexual license) as a danger to the state. As a result, Bacchus, Silenus, and banquet scenes in general were depicted in murals, mosaic, and statuary throughout the ancient world so that everyone could see the paradox of pleasure.

Most early wineries were simple wine-growing farms, or estates, with vineyards, and perfunctory facilities for fermentation and storage. The ancient Roman writer Vitruvius had little to say about wine cellars in his treatise *De architectura* (*On architecture*), other than they should have "windows with light from the north. For when light is drawn from a quarter heated by the sun, the wine will be affected by the heat, and thin."[I] He then describes the spatial requirements for the press, with a room that is 16' wide and not less than 40' long, unless of course there are two presses, in which case the space should be 24' wide. In the late-third or early-fourth century CE, Marcus Cetius Faventinus echoed Vitruvius' brief description in his *De diversis fabricis architectonicae* (*On diverse architectural constructions*), noting:

[s]ite your wine-cellar to face the coldest quarters of the sky. Bring in light through the northward-facing windows, so that cold air from all sides may preserve the wine. For they are all corrupted by hot air. The actual press is to be placed in the northern part of the cellar.[II]

It was not until a century later that the Roman agricultural writer Palladius described the wine-cellar in detail in his treatise *De rustica* (*On agriculture*), giving us a much more accurate account of what Roman wineries were like. He notes:

[w]e ought to have a cool wine cellar facing the north, or very near some shady spot, at a distance from baths, stables, the oven, dunghills, cisterns, water, and other things of a disgusting smell, furnished with necessary vessels, sufficient for a plentiful vintage; but so situated that the gallery may have a place for treading the grapes, built in a higher place; to which, between two reservoirs, which are sunk to receive the wine, there may be an ascent of three or four steps. From these reservoirs let conductors be made, or pipes of earthenware, and let them run around the extremity of the walls, and the casks being placed under at the side, let them pour out the wine into the utensils near them. If there is a greater plenty than common, the middle space shall be

allotted to the vats, being placed on higher bases, that they may not be in the way; or we may place them on the casks at a good distance from each other, that, if it is requisite, there may be room for the curator to pass. But if we appropriate a spot to the vats, let that place be made solid, like the place for pressing the grapes, with small partitions and a testaceous floor, that if the vat should happen to let out the wine, it may not be wasted, but received in the reservoir underneath.[III]

Roman villas such as the one that belonged to Publius Fannius Synistor at Boscoreale, a mile north of Pompeii, contained such wine cellars as the area—at the lower slopes of Vesuvius—was rich in agriculture, especially vineyards. Archaeological evidence suggests that the villa, and several others in the vicinity were almost all dedicated to producing wine (and to a lesser extent olive oil), as they contained press rooms with elaborate piping systems for channeling the leftover must prior to fermentation. Fragments of Greek terracotta amphoras in these villas also suggest that the cult of Dionysus was very much present in Pompeii. To be sure, a small temple to the god of wine could be found just outside of the city walls to the south. Nearby in Oplontis, the villa of Poppea Sabina, Nero's second wife, contained a *torcularium,* or wine pressing room, and the Ville dei Misteri, just outside of Pompeii to the north, was dedicated to making wine, even though the cellars have never been fully excavated. All of this suggests that not only were the villas outside of Pompeii, leisure retreats for wealthy Romans, but they were also very much working farms dedicated to wine production, unquestionably the primary agricultural activity of the region.

In addition to private cellars and wineries in luxurious villas, the Roman world also had many bars, taverns, and other food stands (*thermopolia*) that were commonly found on the streets of Ostia Antica, Pompeii, and Herculaneum, where citizens could purchase wine and other libations daily. These street front spaces, often at an intersection, usually contained an open service counter out front with large sunken earthenware jars (dolia) for the storage of dried food. Often the counter would have holes where similar jars full of wine or other drinks could be placed and then subsequently removed and cleaned afterward. Space for heating was often provided underneath the stand so that drinks such as wine could be served warm. These precursors of the modern enoteca were pervasive in the ancient Roman world and they could be found distributed throughout cities and towns in both public and residential districts.

The collapse of the Roman world, at least in the western half in the late fifth century CE, had little impact on viniculture as wine production and appreciation had spread throughout Europe and the Mediterranean. In the early Middle Ages, wine became an integral part of Christian theology, and so we find that monasteries throughout Europe took the lead in the production of wine wherever climatic and environmental conditions permitted. Though their architectural needs differed little from their Roman predecessors, it is worth noting that ancient pottery vessels such as amphorae had by then already been replaced by wooden barrels. This certainly facilitated shipping and trade, though the subsequent disruption of commercial links through the barbaric invasions of Italy, followed by the Islamic prohibition, and then the establishment of a feudal system, resulted in economic stagnation with more regional wine economies littered throughout Europe. Wine remained culturally important, even if it was under threat, and wine cellars differed little from those of the ancient world. Wineries remained primarily agricultural buildings even if they were attached to a large monastery or impressive rural castle.

By the start of the second millennium, many of the famous wine producing regions in Europe had been established. In addition to the church, a rising population, and the waning of the feudal system, brought about new merchant and aristocratic classes for whom wine was considered a luxury good. Regions like Bordeaux emerged as major players in the international trade of wine, as did coastal cities in the Mediterranean with a bourgeoning trade economy like Genoa, Pisa, and Venice. England became a major importer of French wine with a substantial preference for Bordeaux, creating what is arguably the first generation of early-Modern wine enthusiasts. As wine production, appreciation, and consumption spread throughout the later Middle Ages, the emergence of large storage facilities, as both commercial and private cellars, increased as well. For instance, the medieval hilltop town of Montepulciano in southern Tuscany rests on a series of subterranean vaults where wine has been stored at least since the eighth century. Such subterranean cellars maintained

suitable temperatures and humidity for the storage of wine and have long since been associated with the French word *cave*.

In the early-Modern period, at least from 1400 onwards, many of the wine producing families, chateaux, and names we celebrate today came into prominence. The rise of international banking and the establishment of credit throughout the Mediterranean made Florence the financial capital of Europe. Banking families such as the Antinori in Tuscany, not only had a splendid new palace designed in the center of Florence by the noted Renaissance architect, Giuliano da Maiano, but had since the late fourteenth century been producing wine on their substantial Tuscan properties. The estate of Chateau Haut-Brion in the Graves district in Bordeaux dates to 1525 and was subsequently praised by such notable figures as King Charles II of England, Samuel Pepys, and Thomas Jefferson. Finally, Dom Perignon, the Benedictine monk who "invented" champagne in the early seventeenth century, may have done so inadvertently and over a long period of time, but his fame is nonetheless recognized today around the world at any given celebration.

As for examples of wineries from this period, Andrea Palladio's *Four Books on Architecture* (Venice 1570) provided plans of several country villas and their attendant *barchese* (outbuildings) that functioned as stables, farm buildings, and cellars. Like the ancient landlords of Pompeii, Palladio's patrons were wealthy Venetians whose country estates were both working farms and leisure villas, and winemaking served both purposes. The Villa Barbaro at Maser (ca. 1560), built for Danielle Barbaro—who coincidentally translated Vitruvius in 1556 with woodcut images by Palladio—was designed as a temple-like residence and working farm, with stables, winery, and interior frescos by Veronese that celebrated, among other things, Bacchus and Ceres. During this period, Venetian glassmaking also transformed the art of consuming wine by replacing pottery cups, bowls, and metal goblets, with colorful and playful stemware. Venetian glassware became so popular that it was exported throughout the known world, and Venetian craftsmen were equally sought after. Indeed, Renaissance art, architecture, music, and spectacle looked to the ancient world for inspiration and a new generation of artists excelled in the depiction and celebration of food and drink, of tastes and temptations.

The age of exploration between 1500-1800 not only brought wine to the new world, but also opened the development of viticulture in Peru, Chile, Argentina, Mexico and California, the eastern regions of North America, the Cape of Good Hope in South Africa, and New South Wales (Australia). The Catholic Church played an important role in this at first, as they needed wine for sacramental purposes, but over time, it was simply less expensive to grow wine than to have it shipped. And even though travel made transporting wine in wooden barrels easier, it also made it more susceptible to damage through heat and oxidation. To avoid such ruin, wine started being stored in cylindrical bottles laid on their sides, sealed with cork. This was known as "binning," which led to the inevitable invention of labels, but also made possible the popularity of sparkling and fortified wines such as port. In Europe, the growth of a wealthy middle class gave rise to the phenomenon of collecting wine, with the emphasis on acquisition rather than consumption. The confiscation of church land after the French Revolution also saw the secularization of vineyards and winemaking estates. By 1800, wine was on the cusp of becoming a global phenomenon, but the winery for the most part had changed very little.

The nineteenth century witnessed dramatic changes through industrialization, the transformation of agriculture, the growth of metropolitan cities, and the expansion of the working class. Rail transport of course made a significant difference in international commerce and enabled the spread of wine through new competitive markets. In response, the famous 1855 classification of Bordeaux's signature wines into classed growths—as part of the Paris International Exhibition of the same year—further intensified the wine market's sophisticated quality rankings. This in turn gave rise to the conception of an individual chateaux with a clear identity, not simply as a winegrowing and winemaking estate, but also as a collection of varied buildings that housed the owner's lodgings, winemaking and storage facilities, and agricultural services, however grand or humble they were. Sumptuous classical properties such as Chateaux Margaux transformed the image of a fortified castle into an impressive country house of leisure, filled with antique furniture. Individual proprietors also understood the benefits of having their names associated with their estate, and so properties such as Mouton and Lafite-Rothschild adopted the chateaux prefix as a trademark. Wine regions throughout Europe followed, using the term in various languages, "castello" in Italian, "castillo" in Spanish, and "schloss" in German. The expansion of viticulture in North America, mainly in California, and the Great Lakes region of Canada, as well as New Zealand, increased the already burgeoning markets for New World winemaking and consumption. These regions opted for more agricultural names such as "grange," "farm," and "ranch," or adopted landscape terms such as "ridge," "valley," or "vale."

It should be noted as well that in the latter half of the nineteenth century, the term winery came into common usage, and the architecture of wineries began to develop along the same stylistic lines that were fashionable in architecture in general. One could find *all'antica* (in the manner of the ancients), Medieval, Renaissance, Baroque, and Neoclassical buildings, exotic non-western stylistic variants, as well as rustic vernacular forms, wherever grapes were being grown and wine was being made. This pattern lasted well into the first half of the twentieth century even though economic uncertainty, political upheaval, and the prohibition movement disrupted wine production and trade throughout the world.

The second half of the twentieth century saw modern winemaking reach new heights of prosperity, and architecture became a necessary vehicle for renovation, expansion, and the creation of an up-to-date corporate or family identity. Northern California took the lead in the development of the modern winery through a series of bold investments and innovative designs. Robert Mondavi had a new purpose-built winery in Oakville, Napa Valley, designed by the architect Cliff May in 1966 that resembled the Spanish missions that had since the late eighteenth-century been producing wine in California. Signaling a new chapter in the development of the modern winery, Mondavi's wide-arched entry building with its tapered tower is not just the symbol of the estate, but also the image on the label, forever sealing the success of the Spanish tradition. In 1971, Peter Newton, the owner of Sterling Vineyards in Calistoga, Napa Valley, commissioned Martin Waterfield, who worked in the company, to design an Aegean-inspired hilltop winery in concrete and white stucco that recalled both the Mediterranean aesthetic of the island of Mykonos and the modernist abstractions of such early twentieth-century architects as Le Corbusier and José Luis Sert. The project stood out rather ambitiously from the wood-frame farm buildings that defined most of Napa's wineries. Over a decade later, in 1984, the Princeton architect Michael Graves won a very important and highly prestigious competition run by the San Francisco Museum of Modern Art to design—also in Calistoga—the new Clos Pegase winery and private residence for the Lebanese art collector and businessman, Jan Shrem. Named after the winged divine horse, Pegasus, whose hoof roused the muses to give life to wine and inspire poetry—after a work by Odilon Redon in the owner's collection—the project was conceived as a modern *all'antica* interpretation of a classical Roman villa and working farm. With giant Tuscan porticos, atria, and formal gardens, Clos Pegase provided a colorful and picturesque Italian variant to Mondavi's Spanish mission and Sterling's abstract monolith.

France took notice, and in 1987, Chateaux Lafite-Rothschild hired the Catalan architect, Ricardo Bofill, to create a new underground cellar beneath the vineyards, that would be naturally insulated and less expensive than building above ground. Bofill created a crypt-like cellar in the form of an octagon—instead of the typical rectangular layout—with the barrels arranged in concentric circles around a central colonnaded skylight. The following year, Chateaux Pichon-Longville organized a competition to reconfigure its winemaking facilities in Pauillac. The architects Patrick Dillon (American) and Jean de Gastines (French) completed the project in 1992 providing a masterplan that respected the scale and presence of the historical house, and yet inside was thoroughly modern with a circular vinification chamber with angled columns and a pyramidal skylight. In 1988, the Pompidou Centre in Paris organized an exhibition called "Châteaux Bordeaux," that provided both a historical account of the region and guidelines for future development. Inspired by the recent trends in winery design—especially the Clos Pegase project—the exhibition included such projects as new Lafite-Rothschild cellar and the designs for Pichon-Longville.

In the wake of these extraordinary projects, and of course the Paris exhibition, wineries around the world began experimenting with architecture. The list of well-known wineries that hired celebrity architects since then is too great to include here though the names of Zaha Hadid, Renzo Piano, Steven Holl, Santiago Calatrava, Rafael Moneo, Richard Rogers, and Norman Foster all deserve mention. Two projects are worth considering here as they not only represent the celebrity culture of contemporary architecture, they have also become synonymous with the world of modern wineries and the variety of approaches that are possible. In 1994, the Swiss architects Herzog & de Meuron designed the minimalist stone-walled Dominus Winery in Napa Valley, giving it an enigmatic sense of monastic simplicity. In 2005, the Los Angeles-based architect Frank Gehry provided the Marques de Riscal winery in Rioja, one of the oldest in the region, with the exact opposite. A new five-star hotel, spa, museum of viticulture, and wine shop were designed by Gehry in his characteristically chaotic fashion, with masses of flying elements inspired by the shapes and colors of vineyards and wine bottles. These two projects reimagine the winery as a bold experiment in architecture and landscape, technology and innovation, agriculture and industry, hospitality and heritage.

More recently, wineries have begun to explore less monumental and expressive forms of architecture and have instead embraced more nuanced approaches to cultural landscapes, green viticulture, justifiable building systems and materials, and vernacular architectural contexts. The modern wineries featured in this book fall very much within these categories of responsible and sustainable practice and provide a glimpse into the current state of winery building across the globe by people who have a profound passion for the art of making and appreciating fine wines, and a focus on local history. The care and craftsmanship that is so clearly discernible in the making of these modern wineries is equivalent to the attention that is given to the cultivation of grapes and the wonderful drink that is obtained from the fermentation of freshly gathered grape juice.

In the pages that follow, one will find a variety of architectural projects throughout the world that range from modest private wineries whose sole purpose is to make good wine, to large multi-purpose complexes that fuse wine growing and winemaking with art, fine dining, health and well-being, and agritourism; but you will not find any wineries where the architecture outperforms the simple

process of making and enjoying wine. Though the wineries featured range from traditional to highly modern, this book is not concerned with style as much as it is with architectural approach. In most cases there is a great sensitivity to the existing landscape and historical context of the region in which the wineries are situated, and therefore bridging the gap between the past and the future is a concern of both the architects and their clients. The use of materials also dictates quite often the form and structure of many of the wineries, with wood, concrete, and stone being the most common elements employed on both the exterior and interior. Occasionally metal and other manufactured materials are blended in to give the buildings a distinctly industrial appearance—after all, wineries are highly functional production facilities. Climatic conditions also inform the choice of location, materials, and the necessity for natural light, controlled ventilation, and other mechanical necessities. As in the past, many wineries have underground cellars (caves), and in many cases the entire production is located underground to achieve ideal thermal protection. Yet regardless of the architectural approach, all the projects featured in this book show as much care and sensitivity to the individual functions of wineries as they do to the entirety of the site and related programs, with indoor and outdoor areas, gardens, and vineyards, providing a humane face to the otherwise functional farm buildings. Social spaces for the workers and visitors also play an important role in filling out the projects, making wineries not just places for the making of wine, but also of unique entertainment and leisure experiences.

There is a boldness and beauty in all these projects that reflects the rich tradition of winemaking across the globe, the distinctive landscapes in which they are set, and the creative visions of the owners, architects, and designers who have all brought them into being. It is clear from the projects that follow that the modern winery is a building type whose popularity is only growing and whose variety seems limitless, this despite the relative simplicity of winemaking. Yet, isn't great wine like great architecture in that it emerges from the terroir around it, when necessity and invention result in unpredictable works of down-to-earth beauty. *Wineries of the World* is a story of architecture, design, landscape, and a unique way of living in extraordinary buildings and landscapes that are exclusively for winemaking and for those who appreciate the nectar of the gods.

[I] De architectura, 6.6.2.
[II] *Hugh Plommer,* Vitruvius and Later Roman Building Manuals *(Cambridge: Cambridge University Press, 2009), 61.*
[III] The Fourteen Books of Palladius Rutilius Taurus Aemilanius, on Agriculture, *Bk. 1, chap. 18, translated by T. Owen (London: J. White, 1807), 28-29.*

Photos:
Antoroni Winery by Archea Associati (Page 11), Les Domaines Ott Château de Selle by Carl Fredrik Svenstedt Architect (page 12), House of Flowers by Walker Warner Architects (page 15 - left) Quintessa Pavilions by Walker Warner Architects (page 15 - right)

VINEYARDS

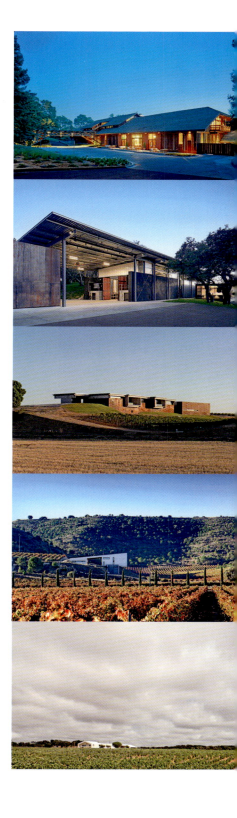

House of Flowers	**18**
COR Cellars	**30**
Antinori Winery	**42**
The Cellar Door	**54**
Joseph Phelps Vineyards	**62**
Furioso Vineyards	**74**
Chateau Cheval Blanc	**82**
Herdade Of Freixo Winery	**94**
Saxum Winery	**104**
Epoch Winery	**116**
Encuentro Guadalupe Winery	**128**
Bodega Zuccardi Valle de Uco	**138**
Quintessa Pavilions	**148**
Epoch Tasting Room	**158**
Beronia Rueda Winery	**168**
Alves de Sousa Winery	**176**
Theorem Winery	**184**
IXSIR Winery	**194**
Winery in Mont-Ras	**202**
Valdemonjas Winery	**212**
Solar-Powered Winery	**222**
Chateau Barde-Haut Winery	**230**
Les Domaines Ott Château de Selle	**238**
ELESKO Winery + ZOYA Museum	**244**
Herdade do Cebolal	**254**

House of Flowers
Walker Warner Architects

California, USA

Building Area:
3586 m²

Site Area:
10,949 m²

Architect in Charge:
Mike McCabe (Lead Principal), WWA
Brooks Walker (Principal), WWA

Project Team:
Maca Huneeus Design, Nelson Byrd Woltz Landscape Architects

Photographer:
Douglas Friedman

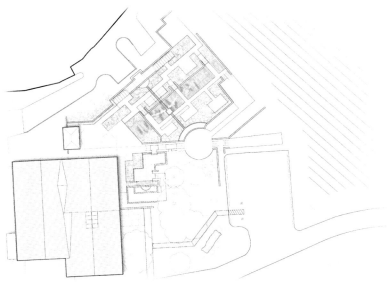

Plan

Flowers Vineyards & Winery is a family run estate started by two horticulturalists, Joan and Walt Flowers, in 1991 on a swath of rugged and remote land on the western edge of Sonoma County, just two miles from the Pacific Ocean. The House of Flowers, designed by the San Francisco firm Walker Warren Architects, located on a small 13.5-acre site just south of the town of Healdsburg in the Russian River Valley, is their main visitor's center, tasting room, and entertainment garden. Completed in 2019, the new 15,700 square foot visitor's center is set in a much more bucolic and agrarian setting and provides what the owners describe as "an environment where guests feel like they are entering our home, experiencing wines crafted without compromise and shared without pretension." The Flowers Vineyards & Winery acquired the property, just off the Westside Road, which contained an existing but deteriorated winery, and therefore a complete renovation and expansion became the perfect opportunity to provide a new intimate experience for enjoying their wines. Remodeling the existing buildings enabled a considerable amount of original material to be recycled, transforming the simple industrial buildings into a new complex of barn-like structures that sit within a redwood grove. Clad in vertical wooden slats and painted black, the buildings recede into the landscape and frame the views of the garden and Mount Saint Helena in the distance. The elegant and rustic minimalist interiors were designed by the designer, Maca Huneeus of the Quintessa family, who also worked with Walker Warner on projects at that estate. The transformation also involved the landscape design firm of Nelson Byrd Woltz, to create new pathways, outdoor pavilions, and gardens framed by rammed-earth walls so that wines could be enjoyed both inside and out. The site occupies the boundary between the gridded vineyard and agricultural fields of the Russian River and is situated amongst the oak-grassland foothills leading up to the coastal redwood forests that surround Flowers' vineyards on the extreme Sonoma Coast. The terraced gardens therefore were designed to evoke the transect of native plant communities indicative of each surrounding ecology. As noted by Thomas Woltz, "[t]he design at the House of Flowers amplifies distinct California landscape ecologies creating a deeply rooted sense of place and a narrative consistent with Flowers' authentic winemaking." The garden complex celebrates the relationship between people and land and underlines the sustainable agricultural production methods that are used by the Flowers to make extraordinary wines, modest vernacular buildings, and exquisite landscapes.

HOUSE OF FLOWERS

HOUSE OF FLOWERS

COR Cellars
goCstudio

Lyle, USA

Building Area: 483 m²	**Architect in Charge:** goCstudio	**Photographer:** Kevin Scott
Site Area: 92,308 m²	**Project Team:** Jon Gentry AIA, Design Principal Aimée O'Carroll ARB, Design Principal	

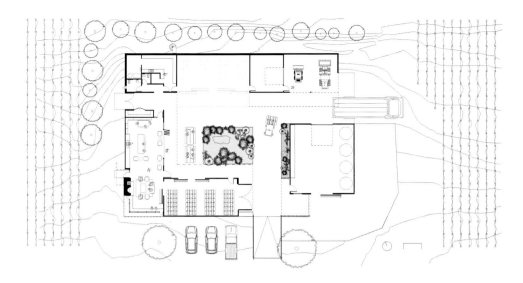

Plan

COR Cellars was founded in 2004 by the young winemaker Luke Bradford as an experimental vineyard on the outskirts of Lyle, a small town on the stunning Columbia River Gorge in southwestern Washington. He now runs the small 22-acre organic vineyard and winery, whose name in Latin means "heart," with his wife Meg Gilbert, and their two young daughters. Their new 5,200-square-foot winery and tasting room, designed by Seattle's goCstudio, opened in 2016 as a renovation of a previously existing facility on the site. The complex is structured around a protected open courtyard and garden that provides access to the winery as well as the tasting room. On both the north and south wings of the complex are the barrel storage areas whereas the east wing contains the bottling facility, crushing pad, and equipment storage. The western wing consists of the tasting room and lounge, with a large corner window providing views over the vineyards and the great snow-capped Mt. Hood in Oregon in the distance. A small prep kitchen allows for further entertaining in the lounge, courtyard, or among the adjacent vines. The complex berms into the hillside on the north and the buildings are all made of wood, clad in vertical cedar tongue and groove board, with a semi-transparent ebony stain. Large overhangs in the courtyard, sliding barn doors, and a massive chimney in the visitor's lounge convey a sense of modern rustic simplicity, very much in character with the relaxed atmosphere of the site and owners. As noted by goCstudio, "[t]he courtyard is the heart of the building. It is protected by the new wings of the winery that form a berm against the steady winds. This provides a calm, protected center for day-to-day operations and a welcoming exterior space for visitors as they enter the new tasting room." The COR Cellars' motto is the Latin phrase "vinum bonum laetificat cor humanum" (good wine pleases the human heart), and the same may very well be said for the architecture of the estate.

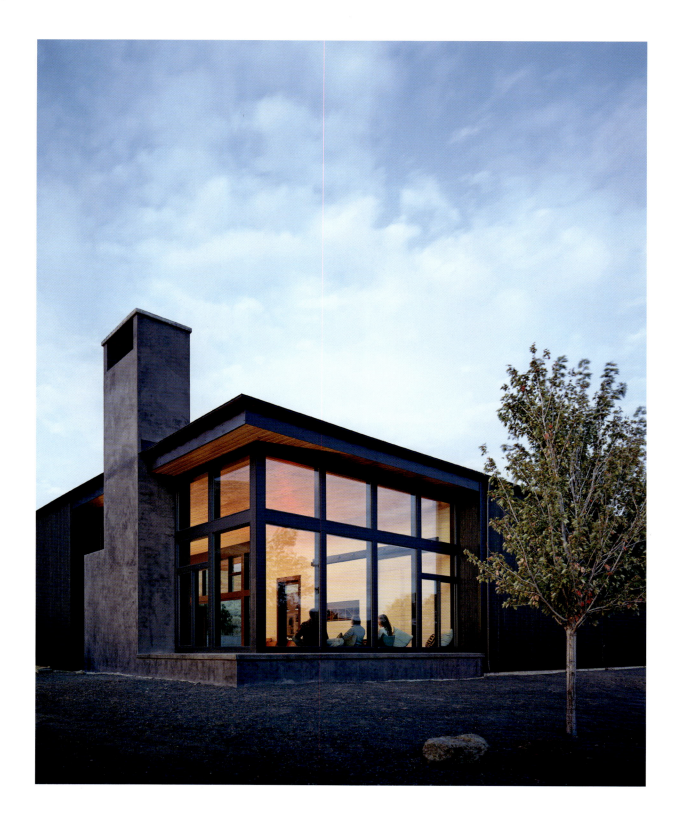

Antinori Winery
Archea Associati

Bargino FI, Italy

Building Area:
28,000 m²

Site Area:
130,000 m²

Architect in Charge:
Archea Associati

Project Team:
Laura Andreini, Marco Casamonti
Silvia Fabi, Giovanni Polazzi

Photographer:
Pietro Savorelli, Leonardo Finotti

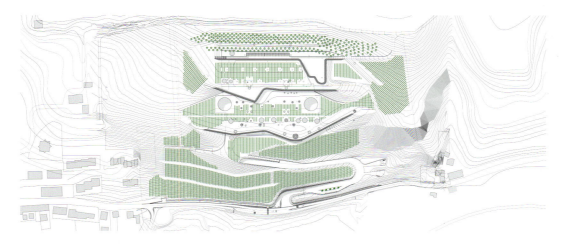

Plan

In 2012, the distinguished Antinori family from Tuscany unveiled their unusual and spectacular new winery in Bargino, San Casciano Val di Pesa, in the hills of Chianti halfway between Florence and Siena. Designed by the Florentine architecture firm of Archea Associati, the colossal 540,000-square-foot winery is the visionary expression of the family's deep ties to the region and their ancestral land, an association that dates to the late fourteenth century. Inserted into the hillside, the invisible building follows the contours of the land and is entirely covered with vineyards, therefore having a low environmental impact on the landscape and offering maximum energy savings. Within its vast labyrinthine expanse lie the winery facilities, offices, a museum, auditorium, restaurant, and several outdoor spaces for entertaining. A series of figural courtyards and horizontal cuts let natural light enter the building, providing visitors and those who work inside with gardens, terraces, and dramatic views across the Tuscan landscape. The heart of the winery is the underground cellar, with a dark and rhythmic sequence of terracotta tiled vaults that convey the sacred character of the secluded space and guarantee the ideal thermal conditions for the slow maturation of the wine. In section, the building follows the slope of the land and is also organized along the production process of gravity-flow vinification, where the grapes descend from the point of arrival, to the fermentation tanks, and finally to the underground barrel vaults. Conversely, the visitors ascend from the parking area to the winery and vineyards, through the production and display areas to the upper levels of the restaurant, auditorium, museum, library, wine tasting areas and sales outlet. Built entirely of locally sourced materials, the winery respects the surrounding environment and the Tuscan tradition of innovation and invention, as can be seen in the dramatic spiraling corkscrew staircase that connects the upper-level terrace with the vaults three levels below. As one of the oldest family companies in existence, the Antinoris are exemplary stewards of architecture, landscape, and the extraordinary gifts of viniculture.

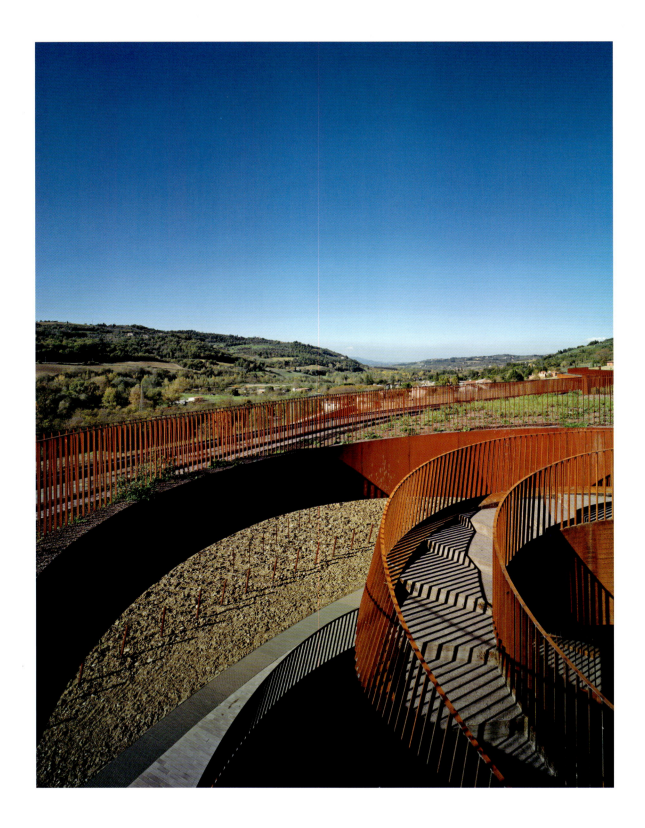

ANTINORI WINERY 47

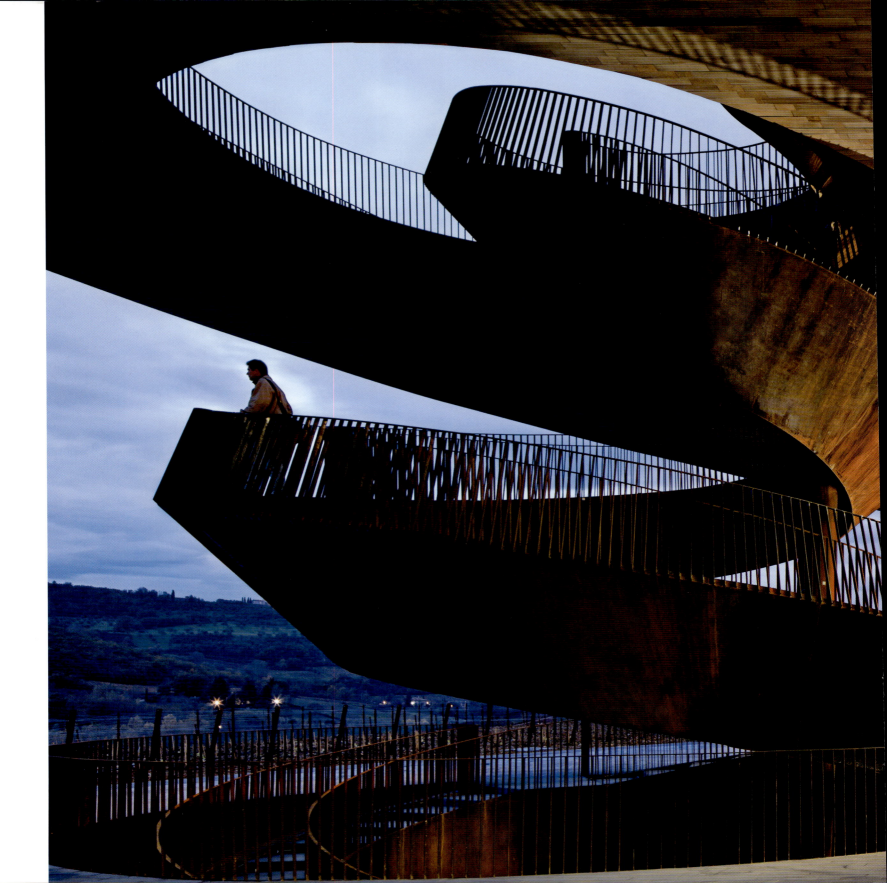

The Cellar Door
Kerstin Thompson

Melbourne, Australia

Building Area:
358 m²

Site Area:
2900 m²

Architect in Charge:
Kerstin Thompson

Project Team:
Scott Diener, Ben Pakulsky, Lynn Chew, Claire Humphreys

Photographer:
Derek Swalwell, John Gollings

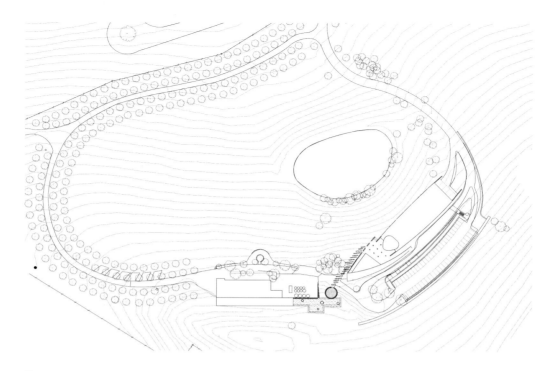

Plan

The Cellar Door is a bold subterranean wine cellar, dining room, bar, and lounge located on the TarraWarra Estate, a vineyard covering 400 acres of farmland in the Yarra Valley, around an hour east of Melbourne, Australia. Designed by the Melbourne architect Kerstin Thompson, and completed in 2016, the Cellar Door is an extension to an existing barrel cellar that seeks to combine an experience of the Australian landscape with "the subterranean charm of a European wine cellar." The program for the new facility puts wine making at the heart of the visitor experience, through the extension of the existing barrel cellar with a bar, lounge area, and private dining room with views of the barrel storage. Visitors enter the cellar through a wooden door inserted into a curved stone wall that creates a circular enclosed forecourt. A pathway connects the main winery building to the forecourt, which in turn provides a discreet view over the vineyards. Inserted into the landscape, the building's roof is covered with plantings of native grasses and shrubs. A group of black cylinders pierce through the roof and provide natural light to the underground vaulted space like a Roman cryptoporticus (a covered subterranean passage). In fact, the cellar is planned as a long sequence of connected spaces beginning with the reception and tasting room, then a private dining room and then the long existing underground cellar, a single aisled long underground hall lined on both sides with wooden barrels. And like a Roman cryptoporticus, the cellar, is warm and inviting in winter, and a place of cool relief in the summer, with discreet funnels of natural light descending from above in the manner of subterranean cellars throughout the ages. The interior employs materials that accentuate the sights and smells associated with winemaking, with textured concrete resembling masonry walls, wooden joinery, and furniture made from recycled timber, all giving the impression of a rustic modern interpretation of an ancient space. As noted by the architect, "[t]he challenge of the project involved responding to existing conditions and forging a new space that was at once in keeping with the character and feel of the existing winery tunnel, while also providing a heightened sense of refinement and identity for showcasing the wine."

Joseph Phelps Vineyards
BCV Architecture + Interiors

California, USA

Building Area:
1579 m²

Site Area:
3000 m²

Architect in Charge:
BCV Architecture + Interiors

Project Team:
Don Brandenburger, AIA, Cello + Maudru Construction, Smith + Smith Landscape Architects, Nishkian Menninger/Monks Engineer

Photographer:
Bruce Damonte Photography

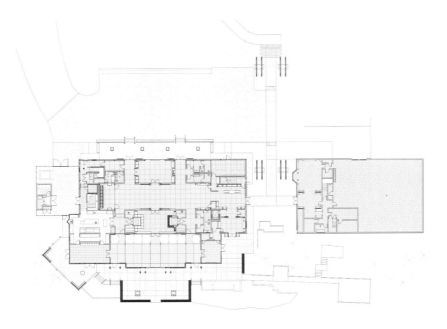

Plan

The Joseph Phelps Vineyards was founded in 1973 by the building contractor and winemaker Joseph Phelps and now consists of 425 acres of sustainable vineyards throughout Napa Valley and over 100 acres on the western Sonoma Coast. The original winemaking facility or "Home Ranch" in St. Helena was designed in 1973 by the San Francisco architect John Marsh Davis, who celebrated the poetics of wood construction and the simple organic buildings of Napa Valley in general. Set within a grove of redwoods, the original structure offered stunning views over Napa Valley and the Mayacamas mountains. BCV Architecture + Interiors, led by their founding principal, Hans Baldauf, completely renovated the original facility in 2015. The new program utilizes approximately 17,000 square feet of the existing 35,000-square-foot building, maintaining the signature exterior redwood design and trellis entryway, while repurposing the interior spaces to include a Great Hall, six well-appointed private tasting areas, a library of older vintages, a barrel room and a state-of-the-art kitchen. In addition to restoring key elements of the original design, BCV upgraded mechanical and seismic systems, and brought access throughout the property to modern codes, while preserving space for future expansion. The project is situated almost entirely within the original building, with existing finishes preserved as much as possible.

The majority of the building's interior was removed, and a new interior floor was added without removing the original exterior structure. A new guest path leads to the original entry trellis, allowing visitors to experience the full drama of this element connecting the hillside site to views over the estate. Inside, the Great Hall was completely transformed from its former use as the winery's fermentation cellar to an elegant tasting room and lounge, with two signature redwood trusses defining the space. The adjacent Barrel Room houses the winery's latest vintages, and the Oval Room contains the estate's historic large oval-shaped barrels and provides western views over the valley. Between these spaces, the Founders Room and Library can display over 1,000 bottles and allow for distinct tasting experiences. Finally, the expanded outdoor terrace and patio offer increased opportunities for visitors to enjoy the wine while overlooking the vineyard and distant mountain ranges. Seeking to establish a new composite whole, BCV considered the renovation as a springboard to provide cohesion and a sense of continuity between the old winery and the new state-of-the-art facility. Hans Baldauf deserves credit for his visionary thinking, as the new Joseph Phelps winery is not so much a renovation of an existing structure as it is a novel transformation of a historic structure.

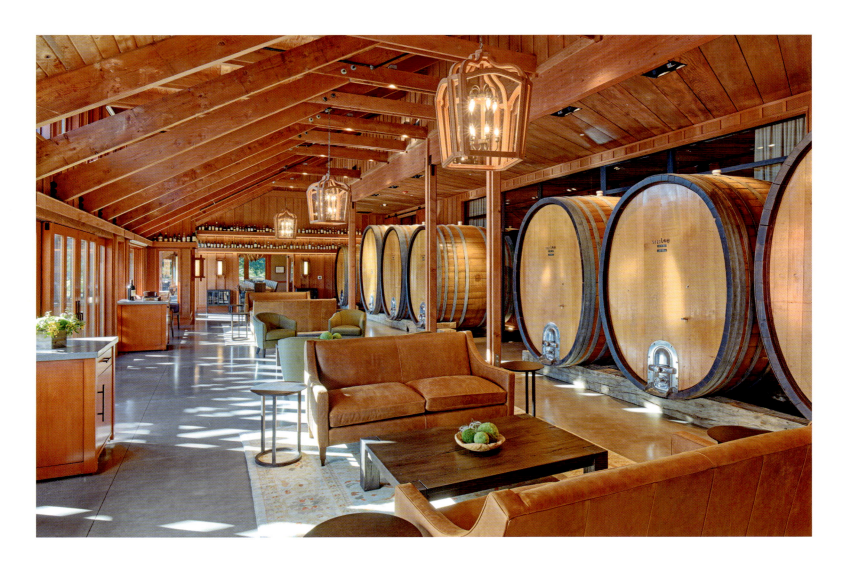

JOSEPH PHELPS VINEYARDS

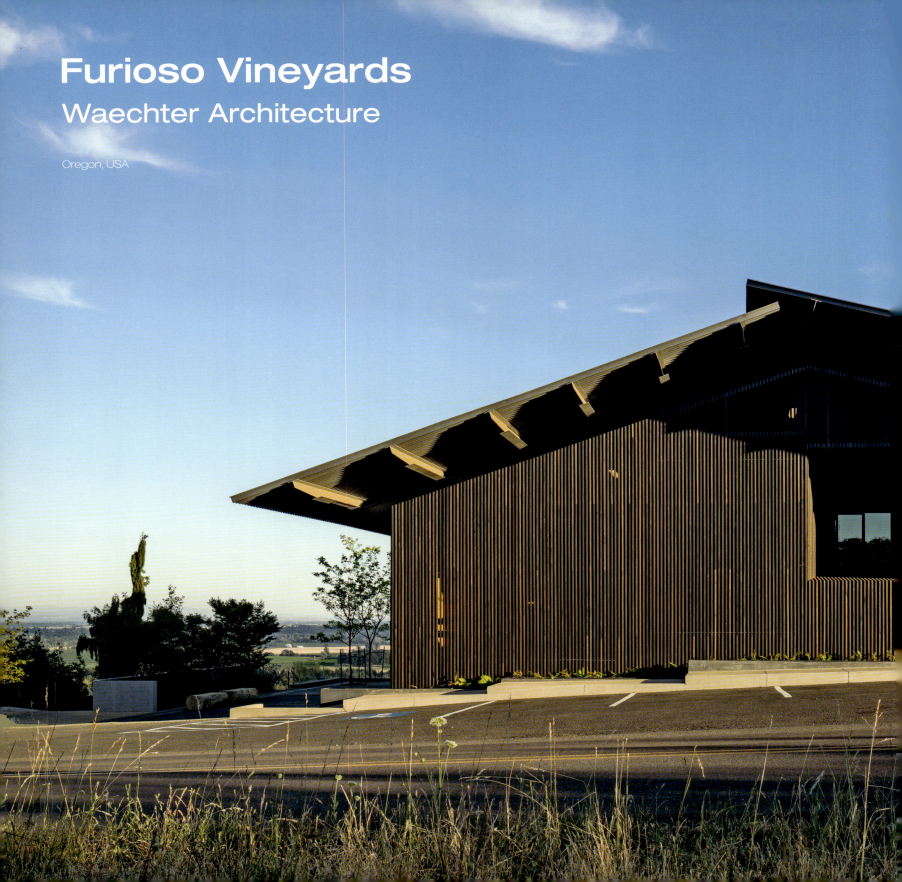

Furioso Vineyards
Waechter Architecture

Oregon, USA

Building Area:
1150.13 m²

Site Area:
98,000 m²

Architect in Charge:
Ben Waechter

Project Team:
Rand Pinson, Ben Waechter

Photographer:
Lara Swimmer

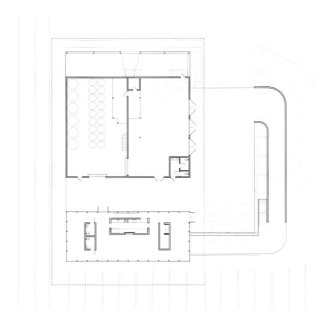

Plan

Furioso Vineyards is one of the oldest wine-growing properties in the Willamette Valley of northwestern Oregon with the original vineyard started in the early 1970s. The Italian American artist and property developer, Giorgio Furioso (whose name in Italian means raging and mad, like an artist's temperament), acquired the small property in 2014 and began transforming the existing winemaking facility from an inward-looking production plant to a new outward looking sustainable winery and visitor's center. Designed by the Portland-based Waechter Architecture, and completed in 2018, the project reimagined the estate, giving each element a distinct and focused identity, while enhancing the viewer's experience of the landscape and the winemaking process. The existing winery was renovated and expanded, reusing its basic structure, while upgrading to new seismic standards. The exterior was re-clad with a screen of vertical blackened battens that extend over opaque wall surfaces and open-air mechanical rooms. During the day, the building takes on a solid appearance, but at night, it appears "ethereal and translucent," as the interior lighting accents the vertical slats.

The new tasting room is open on all sides with glass walls and situated to feel as if it is hovering over the vineyard, providing panoramic views of the surrounding hills. Between the winery and tasting room is an open loggia, a multi-functional covered exterior space that serves as a crush pad for the winery during harvest and becomes a public space for gatherings and events throughout the year. Extending out from the loggia, a new courtyard, or piazza, lies between the existing residence and expanded winery. The southern end of the piazza is elevated above the vineyard creating a dramatic viewing platform. A new shed roof unifies the winery with a singular recognizable form. Made of four-inch deep corrugated metal, the roof cantilevers over the body of the building, letting air and light pass freely between the two. A key component of Giorgio's bold vision for the site was to create an intimate connection between the landscape and the winery. He wanted the building to feel as if it was in the center of the wine-making process, orienting the buildings toward the vineyards themselves and highlighting the sweeping views over the beautiful undulating landscape.

FURIOSO VINEYARDS

Chateau Cheval Blanc
Christian de Portzamparc

Saint-Émilion, France

Building Area:	**Architect in Charge:**	**Photographer:**
6500 m²	Christian de Portzamparc	Erick Saillet, Max Botton
Site Area:	**Project Team:**	
5250 m²	Méristème, Régis Guignard, Olivier Chadebost	

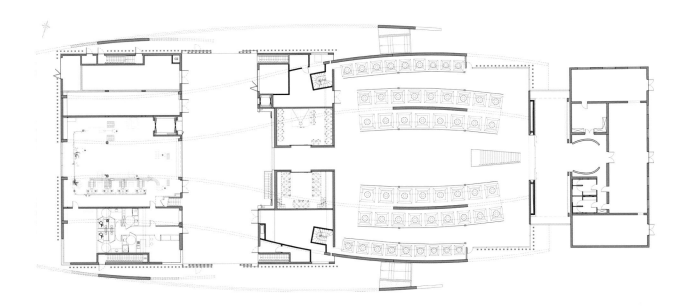

Plan

Located in the commune of Saint-Émilion, wine has been made on the estate of Cheval Blanc since late Antiquity and intensified throughout the Middle Ages. The modern estate was established in the early nineteenth century when the wine we know today, named after a seventeenth-century tenant farm on the property called "white horse," was officially launched. Since approximately 1860, when the main house was first built, the elegant chateau has been the symbol of the estate and has graced the bottle's label along with two medals the winery received in the International London and Paris Exhibitions of 1862 and 1878 respectively. In 2011, the chateau opened its new 65,000 square foot state-of-the-art winemaking facility that includes a cuvier with 52 vats, wine cellars, tasting room, workshops, and offices. Built adjacent to the previously existing winemaking facility, the new project was designed by the Parisian Atelier Christian de Portzamparc, who, in 1994, became the first French winner of the Pritzker Prize. Conceived as a "winery under a hill," the structure functions as a promontory-belvedere that extends out from the château, with a rooftop garden planted with wild grasses and trees that visitors can ascend to admire the beautiful vineyards beyond. Curved white concrete walls transform the otherwise straightforward rectangular plan into two enormous waves that rise from the ground in dramatic fashion. Walls of wood and glass fill the spaces underneath the undulating forms, providing a rectilinear rhythm and color contrast to the otherwise organic white shapes. Inside, the curvilinear theme continues in the fermentation room with large white concrete curved tanks that were designed by the architect at the winemaker's request. The cask storage cellar is below is a hypostyle crypt, with white cylindrical concrete columns supporting undulating beams and a flat slab roof. The walls are lined with open brickwork—like stacked barrels—to facilitate natural ventilation. As part of the Saint-Émilion appellation, the Chateau Cheval Blanc is protected as a UNESCO World Heritage Site, and as such the integrity of the landscape, monuments, and buildings on the property are safeguarded. It is a testament to one of the world's oldest winemaking regions, and to the Chateau Cheval Blanc in particular, that it can accommodate tradition with a bold and visionary nod to the future.

CHATEAU CHEVAL BLANC **89**

CHATEAU CHEVAL BLANC

Herdade Of Freixo Winery
Frederico Valsassina Arquitectos

Redondo, Portugal

Building Area:
1941 m²

Site Area:
2,800,000 m²

Architect in Charge:
Frederico Valsassina, Susana Meirinhos

Project Team:
Henrique Oliveira, Rita Gavião, Diana Mira

Photographer:
Fernando Guerra | FG + SG

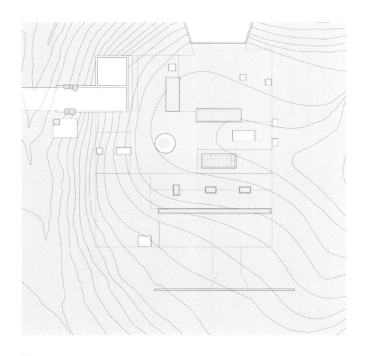 

Plan

Herdade do Freixo is an agricultural company with 740,000 acres of land and 64,000 acres of vineyards just outside of the small village of Freixo, in the north-east of Portugal's Alentejo region between Évora and the Serra d'Ossa mountain range. Established in 1808, the estate ("herdade" in Portuguese means homestead and "freixo" means ash as in trees) is listed as a Municipal Ecological Reserve (REN), with an undulating landscape that accommodates such diverse agricultural activities as farming cattle, arable crops, and cork oak forests, not to mention the vineyards which are located on the property's highest hill. The estate also has a number of archeological sites in the form of megalithic monuments, Roman ruins, and ancient olive groves. Pedro Vasconcellos de Sousa, a wine industry veteran, developed the vineyards with Portuguese and international grape varieties on land he inherited from his father. In 2016, the estate built a new and unusual subterranean winery, designed by the Lisbon firm of Frederico Valsassina Arquitectos, that preserves the rural landscape and respects the production of wine by emphasizing the gravitational process of vinification. This approach also provides a stable temperature throughout the year, which is ideal for the proper aging of the wines. The bold 21,000-square-foot quadrangular-shaped facility occupies three underground floors with a sky lit corkscrew ramp connecting the various levels. A series of discreet openings and cutouts allow natural light and ventilation to enter deep into the interior, providing a chiaroscuro effect to the minimalist geometry of the winery's indoor and outdoor spaces. Vaulted cellars, curved walls, sloped ceilings, and angled surfaces offer a stark contrast to the undulating topography of the surrounding landscape. Similarly, the minimalist décor in earth and wood tones contrast with the shimmering metal of the industrial vats that are used in the fermentation process. The reductive language of the architecture also enhances the scenic effect of the building, engaging the visitor to experience all the spaces in order to perceive the whole and understand the functional hierarchy between the social and industrial aspects of the facility. The estate's motto is "[a] passion for producing distinctive wines and for protecting the rural landscape," a noble mission that Herdade do Freixo achives discreetly and unexpectedly.

HERDADE OF FREIXO WINERY **101**

Saxum Winery
Lake|Flato Architects

Paso Robles, USA

Building Area:
502.60 m²

Site Area:
1189 m²

Architect in Charge:
Lake|Flato Architects

Project Team:
Brian Korte FAIA (Partner),
Vicki Yuan AIA, David Ericsson,
Megan Toma

Photographer:
Casey Dunn Photography

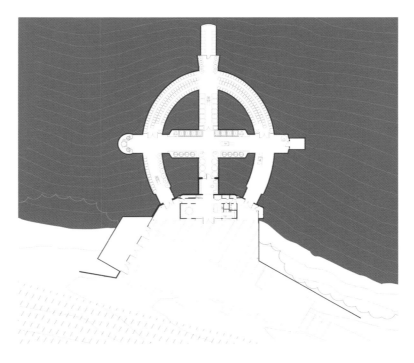

Plan

Saxum Vineyards was founded by Justin Smith and his wife Heather in 2002, on a 55-acre parcel of land in the Willow Creek District of Paso Robles (meaning "passage of the oaks" in reference to the live oaks that populate the area), along the Central Coast of California. The land was planted by Justin's father in the 1980s and since then he has been instrumental in making Paso Robles one of California's most dynamic winemaking regions. The vineyard's rocky soils (Saxum means "stone" in Latin, and Justin's father, James Berry Smith, went by the nickname "Pebble"), steep hillsides, and cooling ocean breezes yield world-class vines that are sustainably farmed without chemical fertilizers, herbicides, or pesticides, and rarely need supplemental irrigation. In 2016, Saxum Vineyards opened their new 2,000 square foot winery production facility, designed by Brian Korte of the San Antonio firm Lake|Flato Architects who are known for their sustainable buildings set in an intimate relationship with the land. Following the minimalist approach that Saxum takes with its vineyards and winemaking, the architects decided to place the new winery almost entirely underground to minimize its impact on the site, and to take advantage of passive cooling. An orange-red-brown steel shoring wall frames the view of a small hillside where a steel and glass entry pavilion with a hovering metal roof projects from the slope. The pavilion also provides shade for two adjacent portals into the winery, where the winemaking process begins at harvest and ends with bottling. Centered between the portals, the steel-framed pavilion houses work areas, a lab/kitchen, lounge, and restrooms that serve the day-to-day operations of the facility, as well as providing hospitality space for private events and tastings. Beyond that, the subterranean winery extends in the form of a cross-in-oval series of tunneled caves that allow for crushing, fermenting, and barrel storage. The underground facility not only conceals its presence in the vineyard and from a neighboring residence, but also uses the earth as a natural insulator. Temperatures in the cave remain stable with only fresh air intake and exhaust circulation maintaining a 60-degree target range. The cross-in-square (or circle or oval), was one of the most recurring plan schemes of the ancient and early-Modern world, and Renaissance architects used the schema for virtually every building type conceivable. This, however, maybe the first time that it has been employed in a winery. It not only makes perfect sense, but it was long overdue.

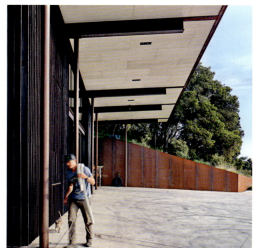

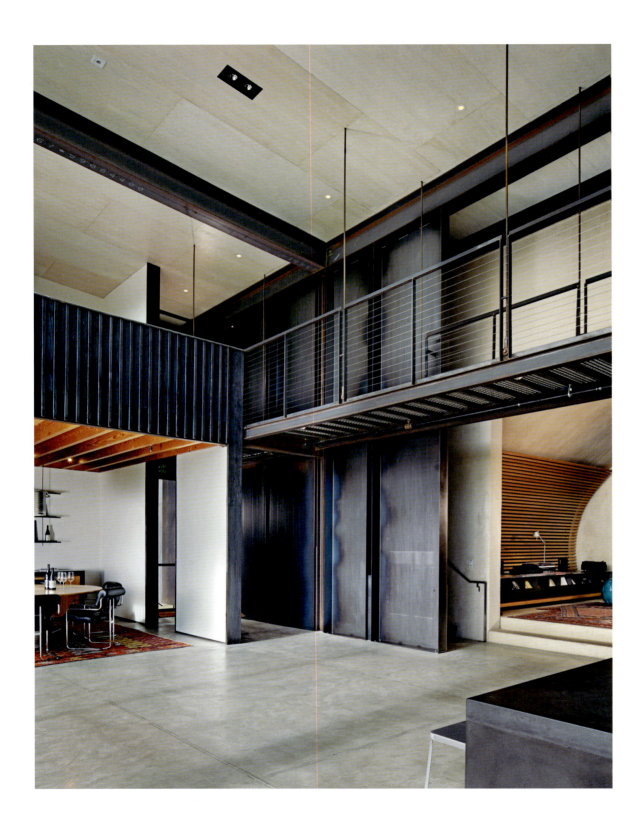

SAXUM WINERY

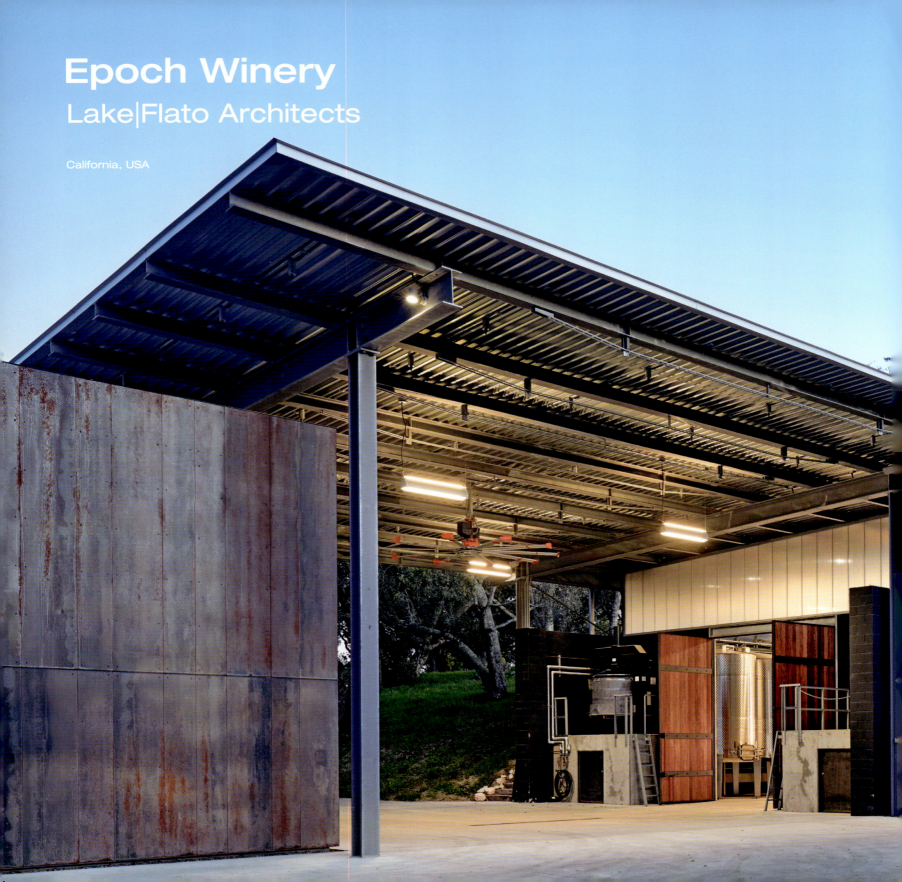

Epoch Winery
Lake|Flato Architects

California, USA

Building Area:
1672 m²

Site Area:
890,308.41 m²

Architect in Charge:
Lake|Flato Architects

Project Team:
Brian Korte FAIA (Partner), Vicki Yuan AIA, David Ericsson, Karla Edwards, June Jung

Photographer:
Casey Dunn Photography

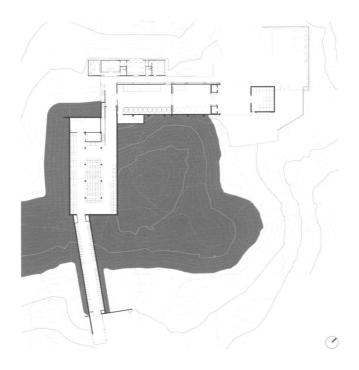

Plan

Epoch Estate Wines was started by Liz and Bill Armstrong in 2004 with the purchase of several pre-existing vineyards and wineries in the Paso Robles appellation, in San Luis Obispo County, just off the Central Coast of California. Concerned with maintaining the legacy of their predecessors, especially that of the composer and Prime Minister of Poland, Ignacy Jan Paderewski, who first planted vines on one of the properties in 1913, the owners set about to restore the various historic structures they acquired and build new ones as well. In 2014, they opened their new 18,000 square foot winery, designed by Brian Korte of the San Antonio firm Lake|Flato Architects, in the oak covered hills of York Mountain, near the site of the oldest winery in the region, started in 1882. The new state-of-the-art facility fits seamlessly into the natural landscape among a grove of live oaks, with most of the production facilities of the winery located underground. As in many other subterranean cellars, the concrete vaulted barrel caves maintain a stable temperature throughout the year. Two strategically placed circular skylights filter natural daylight into these underground spaces giving the sensation of being in a Roman cryptoporticus. Above ground, the new winery incorporates masonry walls that were remnants of the old Stephen's Cellar Winery that existed on the property that have now been stained black. The new winery consists of several spaces assembled under one large steel-framed roof. The intention was to reflect the agricultural aspect of the operation with both simplicity and flexibility in mind. The steel framed winery building houses cased goods storage, a crush pad, open-air concrete fermentation tanks, and a meeting room. Additional above-ground functions include administrative areas, and the well-positioned winemaker's laboratory, often referred to as "the heart of the winery." The entire winery has integrated night cooling to stay in line with the winery's sustainable strategy to use as little energy as possible. A ground mounted photovoltaic array produces 95 percent of the power needed to run the facility, and robust building materials were selected to withstand the particularly dry climate, providing long-term durability and minimizing the need for maintenance. Finally, reclaimed redwood from old fermentation tanks was repurposed to clad entry doors and for custom furniture and millwork. As proud historians of the Paso Robles wine industry, the Epoch Estate wisely looks to the past in order to secure a better and more sustainable future.

EPOCH WINERY

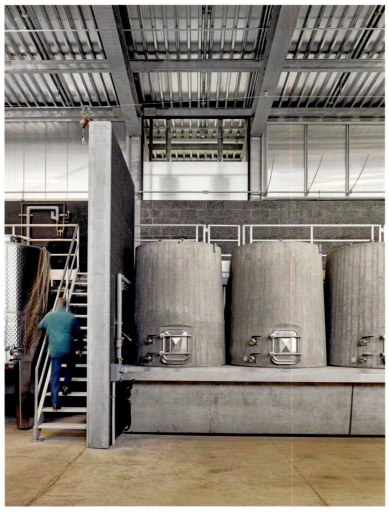

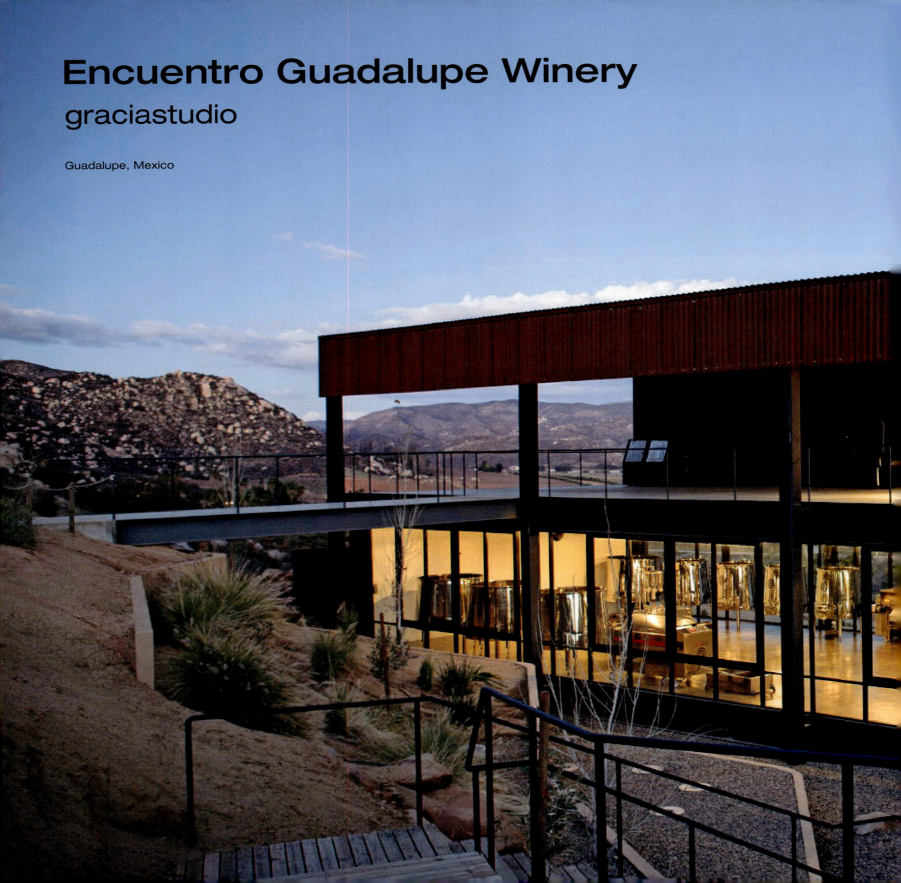

Encuentro Guadalupe Winery
graciastudio

Guadalupe, Mexico

Building Area:
625 m²

Site Area:
940,000 m²

Architect in Charge:
Jorge Gracia | graciastudio

Project Team:
Jonathan Castellón, Braulio Lozano, Valeria Peraza

Photographer:
Luis García

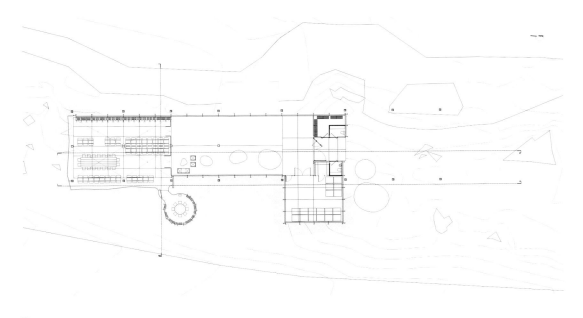

Plan

Encuentro Guadalupe is a 94-acre tourist development in the hills of Valle de Guadalupe in Baja California, Mexico's "Wine Country." Completed in 2012 by the Mexican architect, Jorge Gracia of graciastudio in San Ysidro California, the complex is set in a stunning ecological reserve and includes a winery, hotel, and private residential area. The word "encuentro" in Spanish means "meeting" or "encounter" and the Encuentro Guadalupe is a place of distinct encounters between architecture and nature, flora and fauna, food and wine. In addition to having its own vineyards, the complex also contains an event and tasting area, and restaurants for its guests and general public. The 6,727-square-foot winery is conceived as a two-story steel-framed bar building that is imbedded into a rugged, rock-strewn hillside with the vineyards stretching down below. The main level of the winery is covered in glass and contains stainless steel fermentation tanks, tasting rooms, and a social lounge with outdoor terraces. An upper pavilion semi-clad in corrugated metal offers further outdoor mixed-use space and holds additional fermentation tanks. The cellar is underneath, behind wooden walls made of stacked railroad ties that also frame giant boulders on display as natural works of art. A circular cave is dug into the hillside and offers an exclusive tasting experience. The hotel is formed by a set of 20 independent rooms of 269 square feet each perched along the hillside like pods. One of the aims of the project was to avoid interfering with the land, as the development's philosophy was to respect nature in every possible way. Like the winery building, the self-contained pods are made of a steel skeletal frame elevated from the ground and clad with wood and glass. Made of corten steel which resists corrosion but is not rust-proof, each unit changes its color over time, achieving a unique harmony with the rugged landscape. Inside, the modern-style rooms have minimalistic décor and balconies with floor-to-ceiling windows that overlook the valley. Each unit is conceived as a "deluxe" camping house, providing guests with basic needs, while at the same time being in direct contact with nature. Encuentro Guadalupe is a unique place where the opportunity to encounter nature is presented through a sober modern architecture, that is both visionary and rustic.

ENCUENTRO GUADALUPE WINERY 133

ENCUENTRO GUADALUPE WINERY

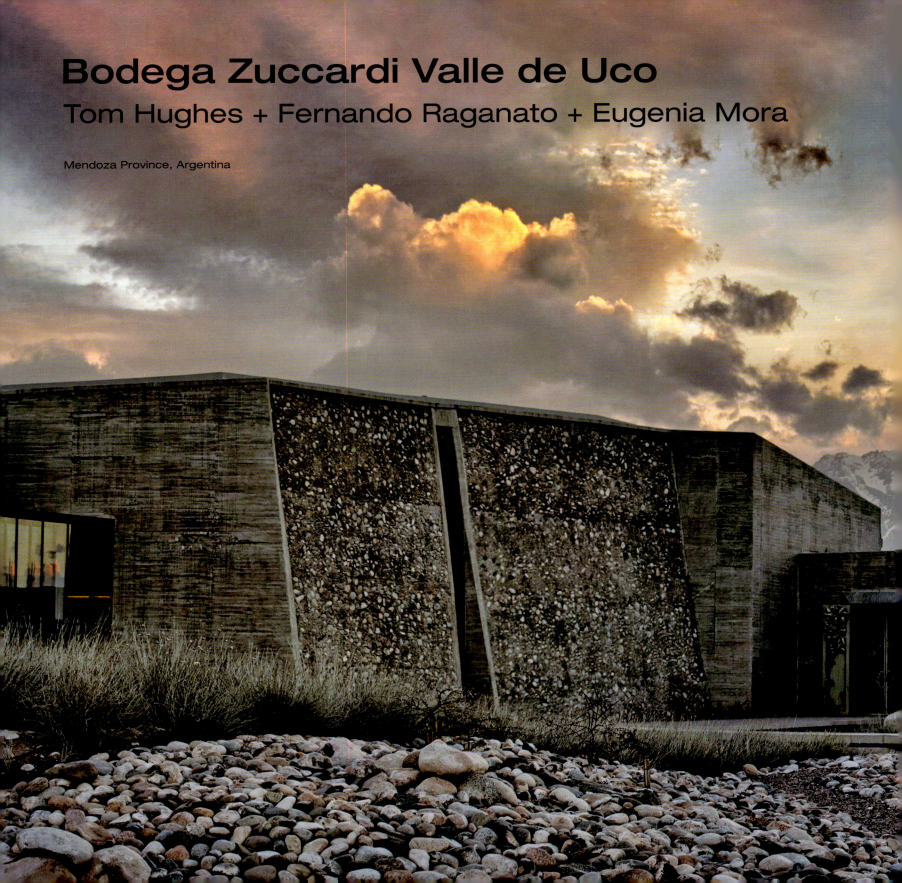

Bodega Zuccardi Valle de Uco
Tom Hughes + Fernando Raganato + Eugenia Mora

Mendoza Province, Argentina

Building Area:
8,841.95 m²

Site Area:
9,587.36 m²

Architect in Charge:
Fernando Raganato, Tom Hughes, Eugenia Mora

Project Team:
Juan Camps, Eduardo Vera

Photographer:
estudio García+Betancourt

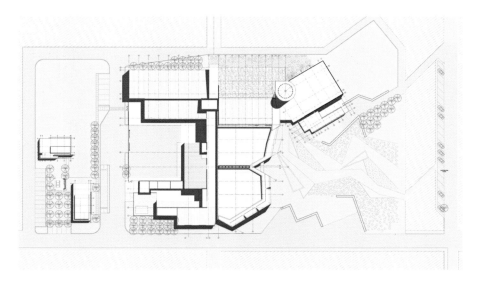

Plan

The Zuccardi family have been planting vineyards and making wine in Maipú, a town just outside Mendoza in western Argentina, since 1963. The Province of Mendoza, at the foot of the Andes Mountains, is known as the heart of Argentina's wine industry, and Sebastián Zuccardi, the third-generation family member to lead the winery, has since 2008 expanded the research and development area of the operation. In 2013, Zuccardi began construction of a new facility in Paraje Altamira in the district of San Carlos, 80 miles south of Mendoza, designed by a collaborative team of Mendocino architects that included Tom Hughes, Fernando Raganato, and Eugenia Mora. The new 95,000-square-foot complex of several volumes opened in 2016, fulfilling the Zuccardi family's goal of providing a state-of-the-art facility for producing the highest quality wines, and providing a distinct visitor's experience. Seeking to integrate the new facility with the landscape, the enormous complex emerges directly from the rocky soil, and resembles in profile the Andes mountains in the distance. The winery is designed along a strong axis which links all the operating areas of the facility. The building also follows the gravitational production process on three levels with fermentation tanks on the upper floor, the lab, production facilities, and administration areas on the ground floor, and the wine vats underground. The process is distributed in a U-shaped plan, organized around a central courtyard which provides protection from the severe weather conditions, and guarantees comfort and organizational practicality. The winery is made of reinforced concrete with great walls of cyclopean rocks, with local sand, and gravel. The various masses rise from the earth like heavy and robust bodies with a metallic dome rising at the intersection of the several volumes, representing the "universal and eternal." The dome highlights the special conditions of the place, reflecting the light of the sun and the sky at different times of the day. A large metal sculpture by the Argentinian artist Guillermo Rigattieri representing the seed—a symbol of origin and providence—is suspended under the dome. Similarly, there is a succession of wine storage and wine tasting areas inside that represent the passage of time and projection into the future. A characteristic Zuccardi motto is "not to strive for perfect wines, but wines that express the place, and the region," and the new bodega complex achieves that in a bold and dramatic manner.

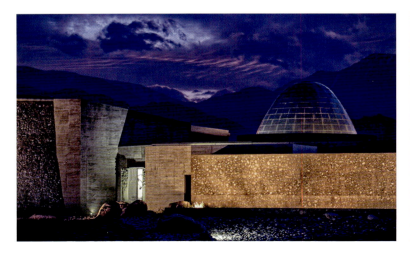

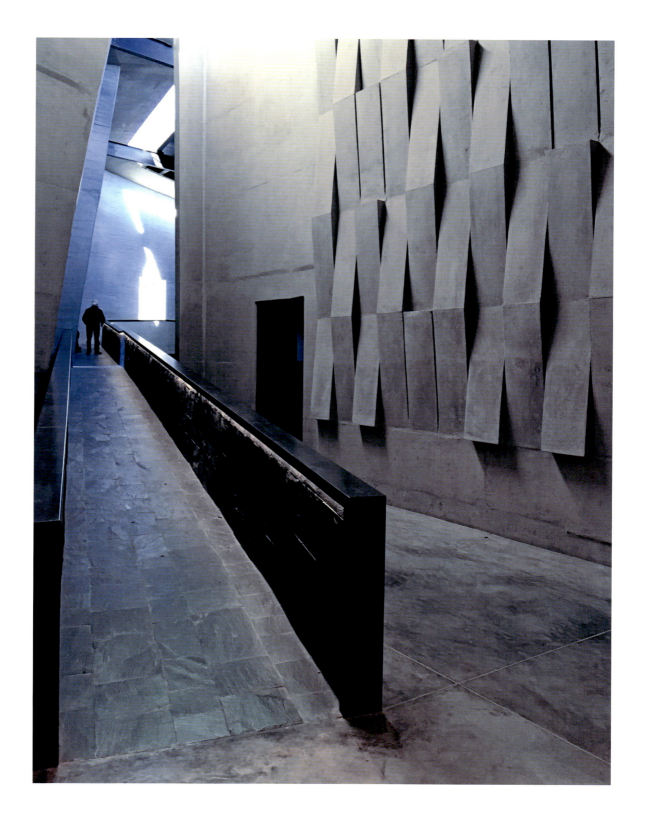

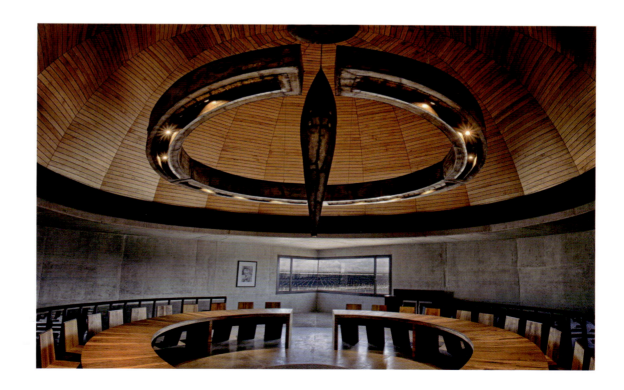

BODEGA ZUCCARDI VALLE DE UCO

Quintessa Pavilions
Walker Warner Architects

California, USA

Building Area:
23.2 m² per Pavilion

Site Area:
1.13e+6 m²

Architect in Charge:
Mike McCabe (Lead Principal), WWA
Greg Warner (Principal), WWA

Project Team:
Maca Huneeus Design, Lutsko Associates

Photographer:
Matthew Millman

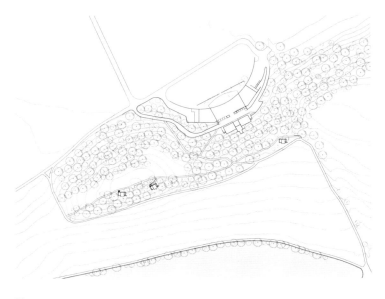

Plan

Quintessa is an exemplary family estate, founded in 1989 by the Chilean vintners, Agustín and Valeria Huneeus, located in the historic Rutherford district of Napa Valley. The distinct property is situated on 280 acres of previously unfarmed terrain that contains five hills, from which the estate's name is derived, though the name is also a reference to the intrinsic aspect or essence of wine. With 40 small hillside and valley vineyard lots surrounding a large natural reservoir named Dragon's Lake, the property also preserves 100 acres of natural woodland, and is therefore rich in the flora and fauna of the region. As a sustainably farmed vineyard, Quintessa also set forth a new era of environmentally sensitive wine operation. The original winery was designed by the San Francisco firm, Walker Warner Architects between 2001-2003, and was inconspicuously situated into a hillside to reduce its impact on the land. Made of natural materials (local tufa and California stone), the building includes an irrigated sod roof, thermal mass and natural ventilation. The curved stone entry wall creates the sense of a "natural amphitheater." In 2014, the architects completed the construction of three private wine tasting pavilions designed along a ridge overlooking the lake to enhance the experience of both winetasting and appreciating the property's unique natural beauty. Designed in conjunction with Maca Huneeus, the couple's daughter-in-law who was responsible for the interiors, the pavilions are also strategically set into the landscape to provide dramatic views across the property and minimize the impact on the mature oak trees that surround them. In principle, the pavilions function as 250-square-foot transparent boxes with almost twice the size of open outdoor terrace space. Made of wood, concrete, steel, and glass, the almost identical structures allow for an immersive, wine-tasting experience in the landscape. Running parallel to the ridgeline, the pavilions have long roof overhangs that protect visitors from the elements while expansive walls of moveable doors help to maximize the openness for light, views, and cross ventilation. With a minimalist contemporary sensibility, the indoor-outdoor pavilions also recall the agrarian barn buildings of Napa Valley, with sliding wooden slat doors and natural stonework giving a great sense of rustic simplicity.

QUINTESSA PAVILIONS **153**

QUINTESSA PAVILIONS

Epoch Tasting Room

Lake|Flato Architects

California, USA

Building Area:
743.22 m²

Site Area:
890,308.41 m²

Architect in Charge:
Lake|Flato Architects

Project Team:
Brian Korte FAIA (Partner), David Ericsson, Vicki Yuan AIA, June Jung

Photographer:
Casey Dunn Photography

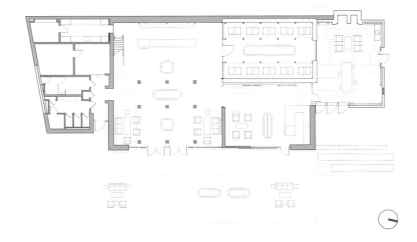

Plan

The York Mountain Winery in Templeton, California, was started in 1882 as the oldest commercial winery of the York Mountain AVA (American Viticultural Area). The property remained under the ownership of the York family until 1970, after which it continued to operate under separate ownership until 2001. The 2003 San Simeon earthquake caused considerable damage to the historic winery building, and in 2010 when the current owners, Liz and Bill Armstrong, acquired the property, they were determined to restore the building and transform it into a new tasting room and hospitality building. Designed by Lake|Flato Architects in collaboration with Brian Korte, now of BK Architects, LLC, the new 2,000 square foot Epoch Tasting Room reconnects the 130-year-old winery to the site and restores the spirit of an agrarian structure in the landscape. The new building is in fact a creative reconstruction of the original stone winery, achieved by salvaging materials and preserving historic features as the "bones" of the building. The existing building was carefully shored and dismantled, with usable materials such as site-fired clay bricks, heavy timber framing, and limestone and sandstone walls catalogued and re-purposed to maintain the character of the original cellar. A new upper story was added and covered by a structurally sound and insulated dual-pitched gable roof that is sympathetic to the original agricultural building in materiality, scale, massing, and detail. A new largely underground addition to the south houses code compliant restrooms, storage, and environmental systems, all capped with a vegetated roof of native grasses. Significant historic artifacts that were relevant to winery were preserved and repurposed, including a large wooden basket press that was suspended above the main tasting area. The architects also reclaimed Redwood from old fermentation tanks to clad entry doors, for wall paneling, stair components and for custom furniture and millwork throughout. Finally, an outdoor terrace and enclosed garden allow for a variety of distinctive and intimate tasting experiences. As great stewards of the York Mountain AVA (the word "epoch" refers to a distinctive period in history), Lake|Flato, BK Architects, and Epoch Estate are safeguarding the future of the region through their extraordinarily sensitive and visionary work.

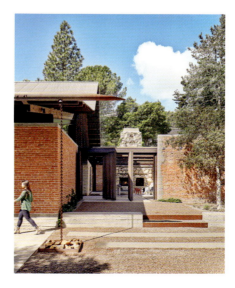

EPOCH TASTING ROOM 163

EPOCH TASTING ROOM 167

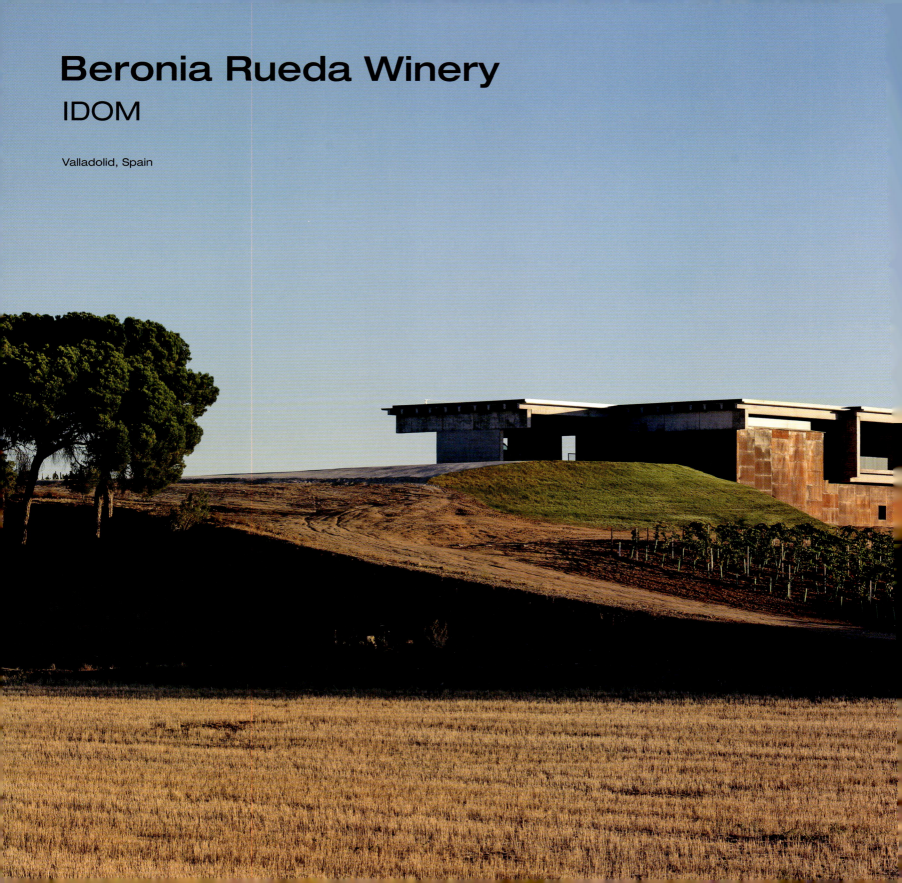

Beronia Rueda Winery
IDOM

Valladolid, Spain

Building Area: 3690 m²	**Architect in Charge:** Gonzalo Tello Elordi	**Photographer:** Aitor Ortiz
Site Area: 10,949 m²	**Project Team:** Borja Gómez, Andreia Faley, Carlos Sambricio	

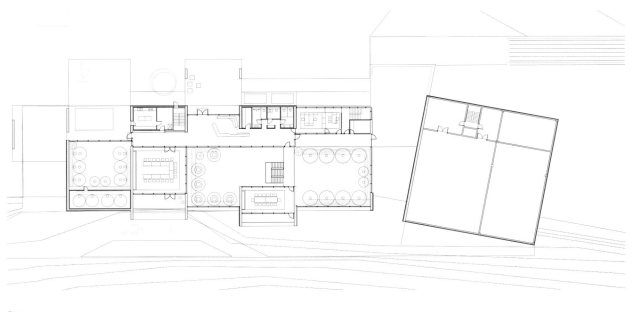

Plan

Bodegas Beronia was founded in 1973 by a group of Basque friends who decided to start a winery named after the "Berones," a third-century pre-Roman Celtic people who inhabited the Rioja region of Spain. In 1982, the winery was integrated into the González Byass family who expanded the vineyards and in 2016, opened two new 160-acre vineyards in the Province of Valladolid, just outside of the town of Rueda. The following year Bodegas Beronia opened a new 39,718-square-foot facility, the Beronia Rueda Winery, designed by Gonzalo Tello Elordi and Almudena García Bacarizo of the global architecture and engineering group IDOM. One of the key aspects of the new winery building was to integrate the structure into the landscape and reduce the visual impact of the building on the site. A hilltop location near a group of trees was selected so that half of the building could be placed underground, and the production and social aspects of the winery could be separated and accessed independently. Visitors access the winery along an independent path through the vineyard, with views of the village of Rueda in the distance. The main entrance is situated at the highest point of the property underneath a massive concrete portico (one of six) that leads to the main lobby from where the social and administrative spaces extend. From there, one can also see the entire production process below, which is serviced by a lower level cut out in the land. The subterranean production area is conceived as a single unit revolving around a central hanging staircase. The laboratory, cask room and tasting room are lined together, leaving the concrete tanks to one side of the stair and the stainless-steel ones to the other. The main structure of the building consists of long-span double-T concrete beams that allow for the open plan, with steel, wood, and glass distributed throughout the interior. The exterior is marked by large projecting bay windows and clad in rusted steel panels that convey a raw sense of earthiness. Finally, several sustainable practices were incorporated into the project such as rainwater collection for cisterns and gardens, reutilization of water for the vineyards, gravity-fed vinification, and reinforced thermal insulation. As noted by Marián Santamaría, the Beronia Rueda winemaker, "[b]ecause of the climate here, you could almost be working organically without actually trying, because this is a very special area." The new winery building echoes the winemaker's philosophy.

BERONIA RUEDA WINERY 173

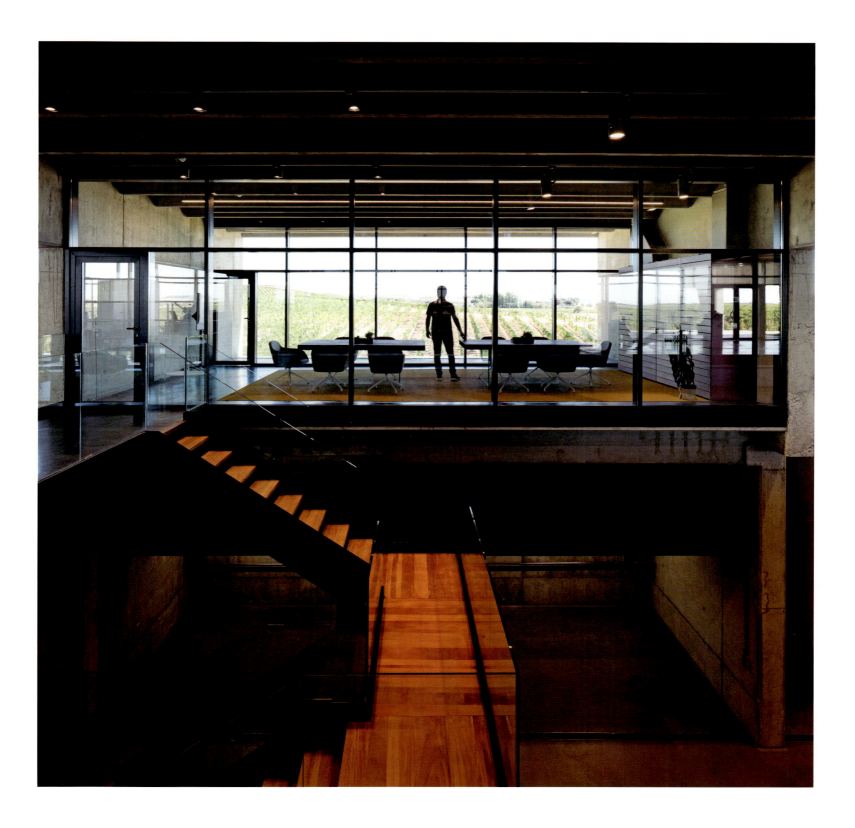

Alves de Sousa Winery
Belém Lima Arquitectos

Cumieira, Penaguião, Douro, Portugal

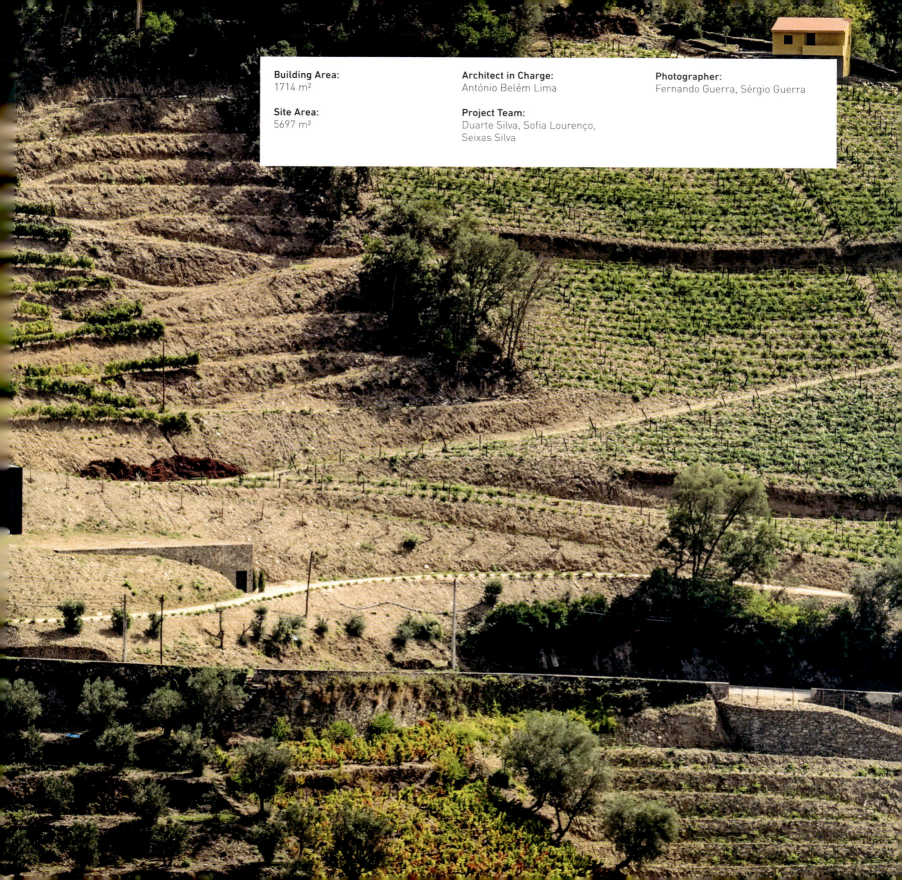

Building Area:
1714 m²

Site Area:
5697 m²

Architect in Charge:
António Belém Lima

Project Team:
Duarte Silva, Sofia Lourenço,
Seixas Silva

Photographer:
Fernando Guerra, Sérgio Guerra

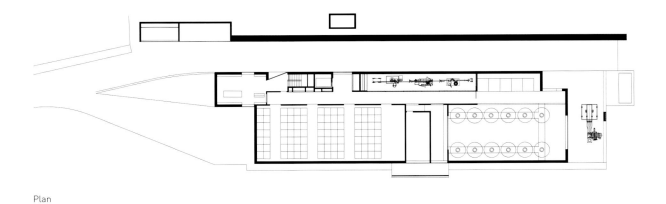

Plan

In 1987, Domingos Alves de Sousa inherited several *quintas* (farm estates) from his family who had been growing wine for several generations in the Douro River valley of Portugal, the country's most important region for the production of Port and unfortified table wine. In 2015, Alves de Sousa opened a new winemaking facility and visitor's center on their Quinta da Gaivosa estate in the *Baixo Corgo* (below the Corgo tributary), a subregion of the Douro valley with the mildest climate and most precipitation. The project was designed by the local architect, Belém Lima, of nearby Vila Real, a firm respected for its minimalist work and subtle interventions. Situated on a winding road that connects the Douro River with the city of Vila Real, the new Alves de Sousa winery is conceived as a thin black box perched on a hillside parallel to the topography, with the simple aim of reducing its impact on the surrounding landscape and providing excellent views across the countryside. In plan, the building consists of two long rectangular levels above an underground black cellar that "hides itself like a bottle." The grape reception area is located in a covered but open space at the southern end of the site that projects over the landscape, visually connecting the Douro valley with the beginning of the winemaking process. From there the winepress, stainless steel vats, laboratory, and bottling, extend in reciprocal transparencies, showing the logic and precision of the gravity-fed winemaking process. Down below, the wooden casks age the wines with order and grace. A tower on the northeast corner of the building houses the administrative offices, staff changing rooms and canteen, visitor's entrance, wine shop and tasting room, and at the very top, a panoramic terrace allows for late afternoon tastings with stunning views over the surrounding valley. The exterior wall is ventilated and clad in black brick that optimizes the building's passive performance in the cooling season. North-facing double-glazed windows and skylights are used throughout to ensure thermal performance. Inside the production facility, the concrete surfaces are left bare, whereas in the visitor's areas and tasting room the walls and ceiling are painted white or clad in wood with black display shelves and black slate floors. A black brick curved staircase mysteriously leads the visitors to the panoramic terrace above the tower. The idea of a "black box" is usually associated with theater and performance, but its extension to the architecture of wine could not be more appropriate as the ancient cult of Dionysus was not just centered around wine and winemaking, but drama as well.

182 BELÉM LIMA ARQUITECTOS

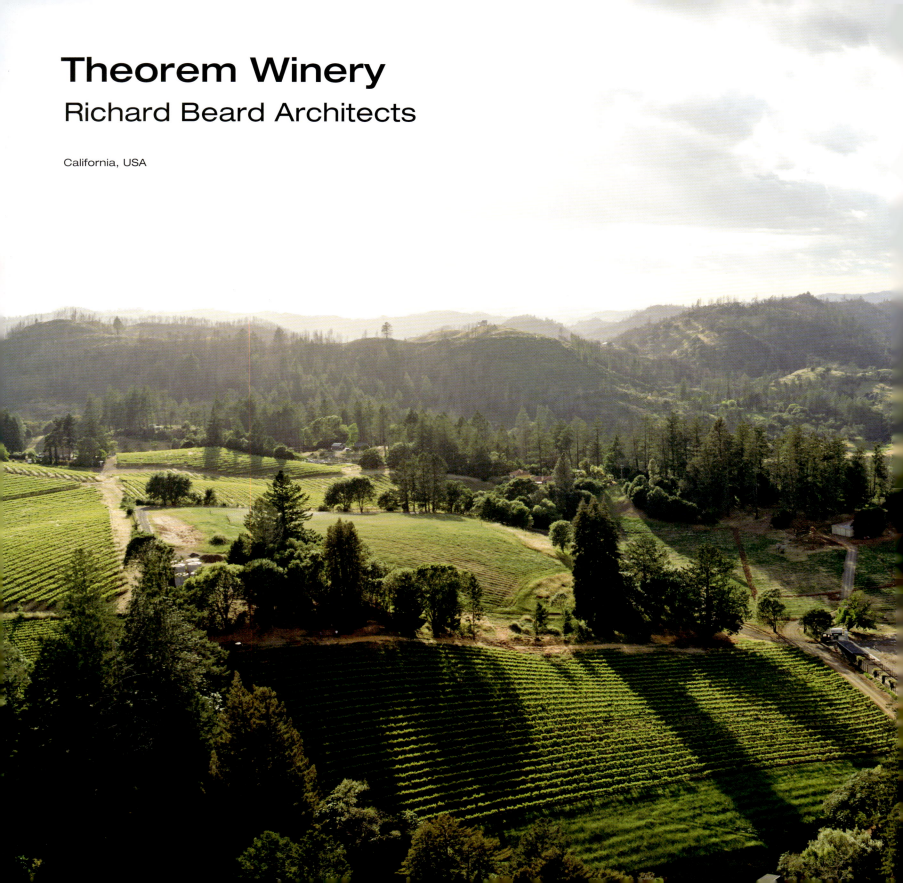

Theorem Winery
Richard Beard Architects

California, USA

Building Area:
834 m²

Site Area:
163,000 m²

Architect in Charge:
Richard Beard, Katherine Schwertner, Bruno Lopez-Moncada

Project Team:
Nicholas Vincent Design, Blasen Landscape Architecture

Photographer:
Paul Dyer

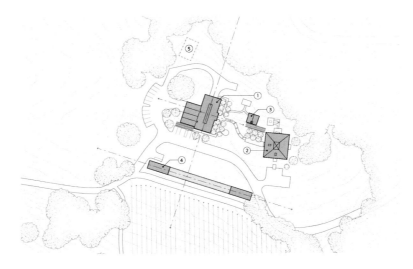

Plan

Theorem Vineyards is located west of downtown Calistoga, within the Diamond Mountain appellation of Napa Valley, California, on a property that houses a significant collection of historic buildings that date to the 1880s. When the new owners, Kisha and Jason Itkin, took over the 60-acre farm complex in 2012, they decided to renew the vineyards that had originally been planted in 1985 (they now comprise 20 acres), and restore the various buildings on the property that included an old Victorian house, a tiny one-room schoolhouse, and a long barn that once served as the farm's chicken-coop. They hired the San Francisco based architect, Richard Beard, to undertake these renovations. In 2018, Theorem opened their new 8,974-square-foot winery building, also designed by Beard, as an "intimate, bespoke experience where hospitality reigns supreme." The winery is located next to the old schoolhouse and Victorian home and designed to complement the vernacular agricultural barns found on the property and throughout the region. Clad in dark-toned wood to recede visually into the surrounding landscape, the complex sits above an underground cellar and provides stunning views of Mount St. Helena to the north and the vineyards to the south. A long arbor/trellis separates the vineyards from the complex and another trellis on the opposite side of the access road provides visitor's direct entry to the winery's reception area, shop, and tasting room. From there a mirror-lined staircase leads to the subterranean barrel room, where exposed concrete walls provide a raw unfinished quality to the space that complements the wooden barrels throughout. The cellar also has rear at-grade access to facilitate the wine production, and a cool consistent temperature that allows the wine to mature. Above the cellar and adjacent to the reception area, is a two-story steel structure barn building with dark metal roofing and vertical board siding. Large, solid oak sliding barn doors, and steel-framed glass doors and windows provide the space with natural light, and visually connect the interior to its surroundings. Additional areas include the crush pad, storage rooms, and a laboratory/office. The name "Theorem" references both the owner's career as a geophysicist and engineer and the old schoolhouse where presumably math was taught. It is appropriate then that the new Theorem winery building is both a state-of-the-art facility and an agrarian vernacular structure.

THEOREM WINERY 189

IXSIR Winery
Raed Abillama Architects

Byblos, Lebanon

Building Area:
1848 m²

Site Area:
25,000 m²

Architect in Charge:
Raëd Abillama

Project Team:
Roger Adaimi, Joy Stephan

Photographer:
Leva Saudargaite, Géraldine Bruneel

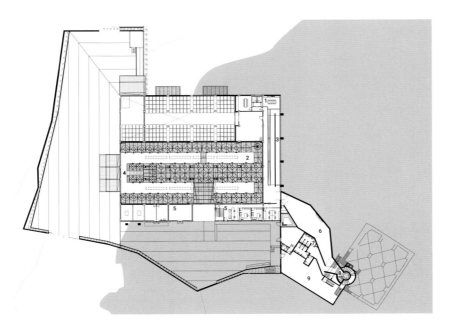

Plan

Ixsir is a Lebanese wine company started in 2008 by Hady Kahale, Etienne Debbane, and Carlos Ghosn, whose name is derived from "al-ikseer" which in Arabic means "elixir." The extraordinary vision of the company is to produce wine from the best terroirs of Lebanon, through sustainable vineyards spread across the country that are maintained by more than 250 families of local farmers. The actual winemaking takes place in a vineyard located in the hills outside of the ancient city of Batroun, where a 140-year-old traditional Lebanese stone house was restored and a new winery designed by the Beirut architect, Raëd Abillama, was opened in 2012. Located on a dramatic site that overlooks the northern coast of Lebanon, with views that stretch southeast across cedar forests, the bold new 20,000-square-foot facility is inserted beneath the ground adjacent to the stone house, creating a novel synthesis between the ancient feudal structure and the modern industrial facility. Conceived as a minimal intervention in the landscape, the old house sits atop a corner of the new facility and the two are connected via a circular stone staircase and a tunneled passageway. The old house was converted into the main reception area of the facility with a wine shop and restaurant underneath the restored massive stone vaults and an outdoor gravel terrace protected by large overhanging trees. The production facility is placed beneath a vineyard roof that contains 22 different grape varieties and keeps the building cool during the hot summer months. Three underground levels contain the barrel cellar, steel vats, loading dock, wine press, storage, and other operational and administrative spaces. The cellar is completely buried underground, providing the ideal equilibrium of temperature and humidity. The vat spaces open to the north west and take in natural ventilation, which is critical to the vinification process. The mechanical and administrative spaces are above and control all exchange flows within the facility. Circulation throughout the new building is via a sloped ramp with large glazed openings that reveal the gravity fed process at every level. The structure of the new winery consists of a functional "assemblage" of both load bearing precast and cast in place concrete elements that recall aspects of the old stone building. For instance, the precast concrete vaulted barrel cellar recalls the character of the manually fabricated stone vaults of the masonry house. Ixsir is extremely proud of its green new winery building that promotes hand crafted winemaking in a region that has been producing wine for thousands of years.

IXSIR WINERY **201**

Winery in Mont-Ras
Jorge Vidal + Víctor Rahola

Girona, Spain

Building Area:
573.64 m²

Site Area:
100,000 m²

Architect in Charge:
Jorge Vidal and Víctor Rahola

Photographer:
José Hevia

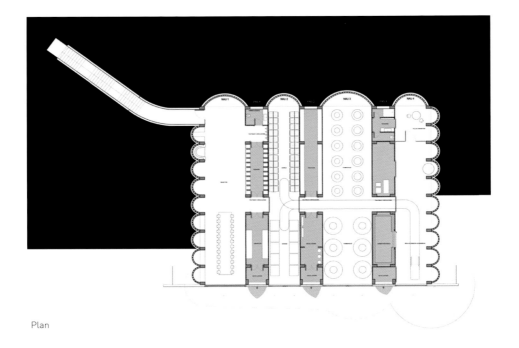

Plan

The Bodega Mont-Ras is a private winery adjacent to a large country house located in the rural outskirts of the town of Mont-Ras, in the Baix Empordà (county of Empordà) of northern Catalonia, Spain. Completed in 2016 by the design collaboration of Jorge Vidal and Víctor Rahola, both architects from Barcelona, the new 6,174-square-foot winery is partially embedded into a hillside beneath a grass roof, with only one façade open to view. The program for the winery is developed around four themes: the relationship between the existing house and the available land for the winery; the humidity of the soil that helps in the maturing of the wine; the sensual quality of the spaces; and the functional and structural aspects of the building. The wine production occurs in four unequal vaulted spaces that move from right to left with three smaller flat-roofed service bays between them. The first space houses the farming equipment and tools for the vineyards with laboratories and freezers separating it from the next vaulted space which holds the concrete and steel vats. This bay is the widest and therefore has the highest space as the vats need to be serviced from above as well as below. The third bay is for barrel storage and bottling, and the last bay is the tasting area with a visible display of the bottles that are ready to be opened. The four bays are open to the service yard and vineyards, and a private tunnel from the final bay connects directly to the main house. The embedded structure helps with the production and maturation of the wine. The surrounding earth maintains an ideal temperature throughout the facility. The deep barrel-vaulted spaces also help with sound abortion, and semi-circular light wells on the perimeter allow for natural light and ventilation to penetrate the space gracefully. The building functions as a platform beneath the earth. Its roof garden lies on top of the concrete vaults that are structurally calculated as sections of hyperbolic arches resting on heavy concrete piers. At the same time the platform collects and retains water for re-use throughout the facility. Brick walls fill the spaces between the piers and along the perimeter. Finally, sliding wooden barn doors, and revolving shutters in the lunettes of the arches, give the complex a subtle contrast of materials that are both natural and earthy. The architects have noted that the project has something Roman about it, like thermal baths that are made of brick vaults, with curved surfaces, and a dramatic contrast of light and shadow.

WINERY IN MONT-RAS

Valdemonjas Winery
Agag+Paredes

Valladolid, Spain

Building Area:
861 m²

Site Area:
94,300 m²

Architect in Charge:
Ana Agag and Silvia Paredes

Photographer:
Ramon Jimenez

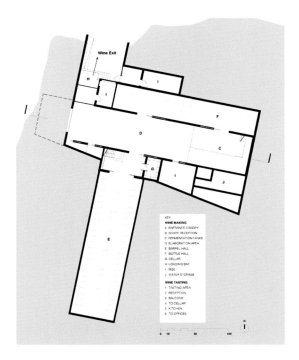

Plan

Bodega Valdemonjas is a 23-acre estate owned by the Moyano-Agüera family in the Ribera del Duero DOP (designation of origin), in Quintanilla de Arriba (Valladolid), Spain. Located next to the famed Vega Sicilia estate, the vineyards were planted in the 1990s on land called "Pago de Valdemonjas" (property of the valley of nuns) which date to the middle ages when Cistercian monks first brought vines to the region. In 2012, the family hired two rising Spanish architects from London, Ana Agag and Silvia Paredes, both formerly with Foster + Partners, to design a new 9,267-square-foot winery which opened in 2015. Perched on a hilltop and partially cantilevered above the slope, the new winery was conceived as a signature landmark that could be seen from afar. Its bold and stunning shape, a sculptural box with a single-sloped roof, is streaked with horizontal lines and pierced by an assortment of seemingly random windows and openings. The unique box houses two of the most important aspects of the winery: at one end the grape reception (the beginning of the process of winemaking) and at the other, projecting over the landscape, the wine tasting lounge, terrace, and display areas with direct access to the barrel cellar below (the end of the process).

In between is a large cutout courtyard, or entry canopy, that provides access to both sides of the facility and is accentuated with a colorful abstract mural that resembles clusters of grapes during harvest. Beneath the projecting box are the production areas with a central hall that houses the fermentation tanks and elaboration areas. On one side of the central space is the bottling area and loading bay that is cut out from the hill, whereas on the other side is the brick vaulted barrel cellar set perpendicular to the general arrangement—running parallel with the hillside—and terminated by another abstract mural that continues the harvest theme. The building responds to several environmental principles that the owners insisted upon. The sloping roof contains photovoltaic panels to capture solar energy, yet also allows for rainwater collection leading to an underground reservoir. The western façade has been equipped with passive solar control systems, and interior spaces enjoy natural ventilation throughout. Finally, the underground production facility maintains ideal thermal protection for the making and aging of the wine. The Valdemonjas winery is a small, self-sufficient, and powerful symbol of what a visionary family can accomplish with land, vineyards, and architecture.

VALDEMONJAS WINERY

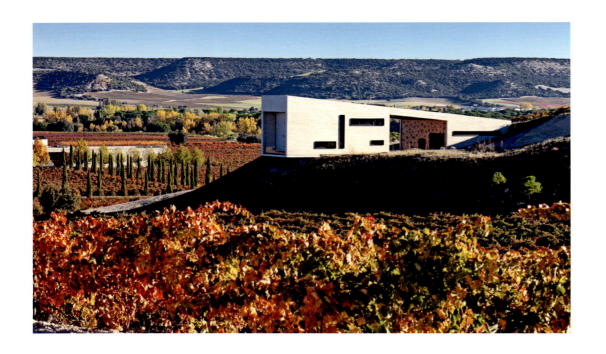

Solar-Powered Winery
Munarq Arquitectes

Majorca, Spain

Building Area: 1300 m²	**Architect in Charge:** Pau Munar, Rafel Munar	**Photographer:** Adria Goula
Site Area: 50,000 m²	**Project Team:** Munarq	

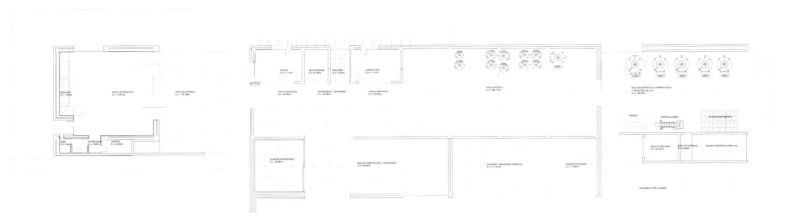

Plan

Bodega Son Juliana was started by the German businessman, Günther Zimmer, in 2013, on a 17-acre flat site on the island of Mallorca, between the towns of Santa Eugènia and Biniali. Zimmer was famous for having invented and patented the brake pad, but he had no experience in winemaking. His intuition, however, was to do things naturally and sustainably, and so in 2016 he opened a 100 percent solar-powered winery on the property that was designed by the Mallorca based firm of Munarq Arquitectes. The new 14,000-square-foot winery is set parallel to the dramatic Tramuntana mountains in the distance, creating a distinct relationship between the flat site and the rugged horizon. Consisting of two structures, a small square wine tasting room and shop, and a larger rectangular production facility, the two buildings share a trellis-covered entry court with views over the vineyards. The linear shape of the production facility responds to the making of the wine. The grapes enter from the eastern end of the facility under a covered porch where they are stripped and pressed and then moved to the stainless-steel fermentation tanks in the center of the building. The barrel cellar is located entirely underground and surrounded by stone retaining walls. It is connected to the two structures above via staircases. The bottling and labeling occurs at the western end of the production facility before being stored in a cool room adjacent to the courtyard and visitor's lounge, completing the winemaking circuit. The winery works with 100 percent renewable energy (solar and wind turbine), passive ventilation, and geothermal systems. The buildings are made entirely of stone with cork-lined insulation on the single-slope south-facing roof, and the underground cellar maintains an ideal temperature and humidity for the aging of wine. As noted by Zimmer, "[f]rom the beginning, our ambition was to apply natural cultivation methods to the cultivation and aging of the wine. We renounce the use of chemical products in crops and carry out a laborious manual care of the land."

SOLAR-POWERED WINERY

Chateau Barde-Haut Winery

Nadau Lavergne Architects

Saint-Christophe-des-Bardes, France

Building Area:
1870 m²

Site Area:
1050 m²

Architect in Charge:
Nadau Architecture

Photographer:
Philippe Caumes

Plan

Chateau Barde-Haut is a 42-acre estate located in the commune of Saint Christophe des Bardes, on the far-eastern side of the Saint-Émilion appellation. Owned by Hélène Garcin and Patrice Lévèque—who also run Clos l'Eglise in Pomerol, Château Poesia in Saint-Émilion, and Poesia in Mendoza, Argentina—Chateau Barde-Haut is a 250-year-old property that the owners acquired in 2000. In 2012, the family completed a massive renovation of their existing cellar, under the direction of the French architects Jérémy Nadau and Vincent Lavergne, who run studios in Paris and Bordeaux. The existing winery contained three nineteenth-century stone structures in the form of simple sheds, two of which were side-by-side and the other free-standing. These were restored and two new buildings were added to the property: the first, a large production facility inserted between the existing stone structures; and the second, a free-standing shed building at the back with a terrace that overlooks the vineyards. The inserted building includes the wine-making facility, fermentation tanks, shop, and the reception area, whereas the former free-standing building was transformed into the main barrel cellar. The reception area also contains a glass-enclosed barrel display space underneath an upper-level great hall that is entirely clad in vertical wooden slats. The two other stone buildings house administrative offices, lodging, and bottle storage. The rear building consists of 4 spaces underneath a grass-covered accordion roof with solar panels that houses in sequence, the workshop, staff changing rooms, material storage, and finally a wood-clad vintner's lounge that opens out to the terrace. With a focus on green and environmentally conscious practice, the wine is moved by gravity, with vinification occurring in a mix of wooden tanks, stainless steel, and concrete vats. Additional sustainable features include filters to collect, clean, and recycle rainwater, and a small wind turbine that creates outdoor lighting. The new buildings employ concrete, steel and wood throughout, and both are covered on the exterior with rusted sheets of corten steel whose color changes according to the season, providing a sensuously weathered yet minimalist appearance. The use of renewable resources has been one of the main priorities in the renovation, design, and management of Chateau Barde-Haut, making it an exemplary model of responsible and modern winemaking.

CHATEAU BARDE-HAUT WINERY

Les Domaines Ott Château de Selle
Carl Fredrik Svenstedt Architect

Taradeau, France

Building Area:
4200 m²

Site Area:
600,000 m²

Architect in Charge:
Carl Fredrik Svenstedt

Project Team:
Tae In Kim, Camille Jacoulet, Thomas Carpentier, Clément Niau

Photographer:
Dan Glasser, Herve Abbadie, Boris Lefevre

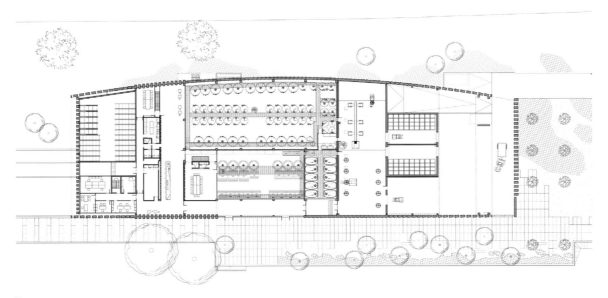

Plan

Domaines Ott is a family-run winery in the rolling hills of Provence, France, that was started in 1896 by an Alsatian agronomist, Marcel Ott, who was fascinated by the landscape of Taradeau, where in 1912 he acquired his first estate which he named Chateau de Selle (meaning saddle). Today, Domaines Ott owns three estates, and in 2017, they opened their stunning new winery and visitor's center on the property of the Chateau. Designed by the Swedish-Canadian architect, Carl Fredrik Svenstedt, who is based in Paris, the new 45,000-square-foot facility is clad entirely in stone extracted from local Roman quarries, allowing the building to emerge from the landscape. Inspired by the nearby Abbaye du Thoronet, a late-twelfth and early-thirteenth century Cistercian monastery that coincidentally also inspired the twentieth-century French architect Le Corbusier for his design of the convent at La Tourette, the new winery is an imposing presence on the Provencal landscape. The simple geometric building oriented along the north/south axis with a bowed façade facing east, is partially embedded into the landscape to allow natural gravitational flow and a coherent linear process that culminates in the underground cellar. This also allows for the building to achieve a consistent internal temperature and humidity that is optimal for winemaking. The facility is serviced from the south whereas visitors arrive from the north and enter from above with views over the entire production process. The exterior stone walls are a combination of massive cyclopean pillars that rise 10 meters and 1-square-meter blocks that delicately overlap, twist, and dissolve. In doing so, the walls frame the winemaking process, shelter the wine and visitors, and allow for natural light and ventilation to permeate the interior spaces. As noted by the architect, "[t]he sun warms the surface of the stone, soft as sand. Visitors can measure themselves against the human scale of the blocks, close enough to be touched. It is a meeting of the senses. What remains are the pines, the vines and the mountain." Inside, the building is minimally articulated in materials and color with concrete columns, beams, and slabs, stainless steel fermentation tanks, oak barrels, and stone detailing in the visitor's areas. Wooden furniture and zig-zag walls in the reception area and tasting room, provide a touch of warmth to the otherwise cool structure. The story of Domaines Ott is one of passion, and their new winery and visitor's center reflects the family's 120-year commitment to—and love of—the site.

ELESKO Winery + ZOYA Museum
Cakov + Partners

Modra, Slovakia

Building Area:
5400 m²

Site Area:
25,000 m²

Architect in Charge:
cakov + partners | Kalin Cakov, Metodiy Monev, Ján Obušek

Project Team:
Jan Obušek, Miloš Djura ka, Martin Boška

Photographer:
Tomaš Manina, Juraj Bartoš

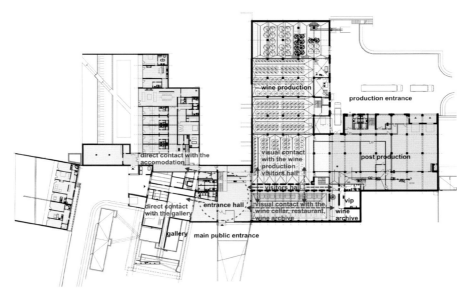

Plan

Elesko is a modern winery with 272 acres of vineyards near the historic town of Modra, in the Malokarpatská or "Lesser Carpathian" region of Slovakia, the most important wine-growing area of the country. In 2009, Elesko opened their new 58,000-square-foot multi-purpose facility or "wine park," designed by the Bratislava architecture and design firm, Cakov + Partners, that houses wine production, an art museum, restaurant, shop, offices, staff accommodation, and a hotel with spa and hunting room. In plan, the complex consists of two main volumes, a large production facility and a slightly bent bar building that houses the museum and guest accommodations, with an entrance hall in between them that offers wine tastings. The entrance hall also provides access to the restaurant directly above it which in turn offers direct contact with the winery and gallery wings. A small courtyard behind the entrance hall, extends out from the restaurant and provides space for outdoor entertaining. The winery production facility is designed as a compact unit and is carefully immersed into the site and entirely covered by a green roof with punctured skylights, ensuring that an ideal temperature and humidity balance is achieved. Visually, the winery is conceived as an "archaic concrete prism" with a sloped rock wall covered in green which creates a protective barrier for the production and barrel aging areas. Service to the winery is provided from a sunken court in the northeast corner of the facility. The administration offices, the owner's VIP lounge, a tasting salon, and archives are also located in the production wing. The museum is the signature element of the project, and an extension of the Zoya Gallery in Bratislava. Dedicated to the exhibition of twentieth-century art, the museum is a bold white rectangular form that bends near the middle and has open glass walls at both the north and south facades. The side walls are pierced with vertical strips of glass that stretch diagonally across the roof as zig-zagging skylights. Underneath the museum, the guest accommodations and staff quarters wrap around another outdoor sunken court and are both covered with grass roofs. Elesko's philosophy is to integrate organic viticultural processes, which have been handed down through the ages, with modern architecture, technology, and hospitality.

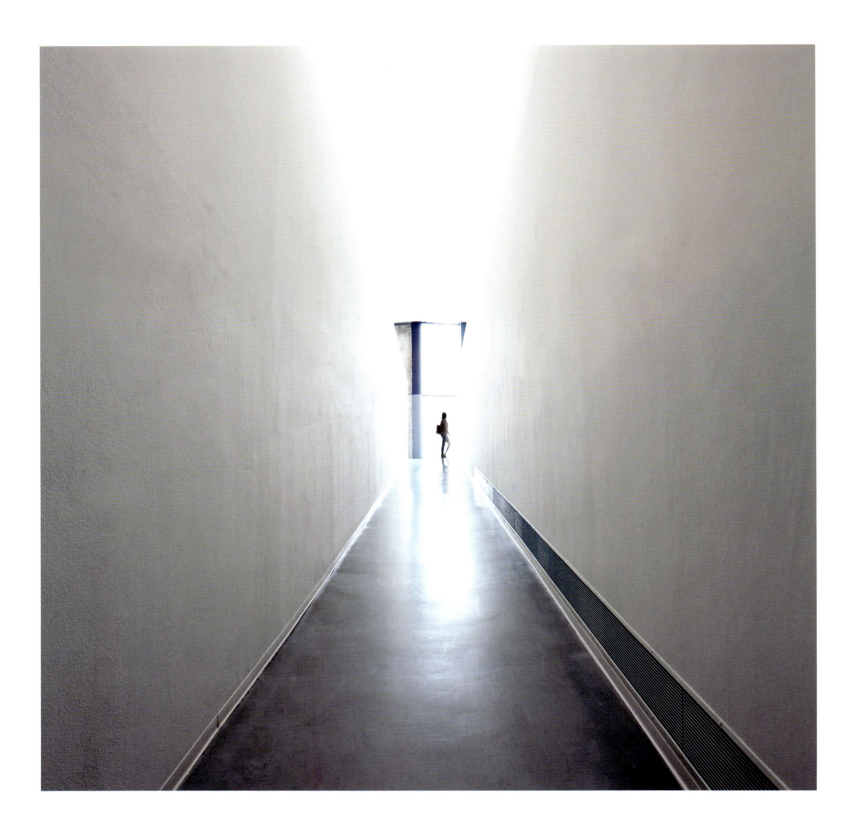

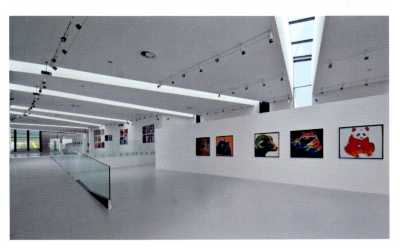

ELESKO WINERY + ZOYA MUSEUM

Herdade do Cebolal
Ribeiro de Carvalho arquitectos

Santiago do Cacém, Portugal

Building Area:
1500 m²

Site Area:
200,000 m²

Architect in Charge:
Ribeiro de Carvalho Arquitectos

Project Team:
Miguel Ribeiro de Carvalho, João Ribeiro de Carvalho, Pedro Machado, Carlos Araújo

Photographer:
Francisco Nogueira

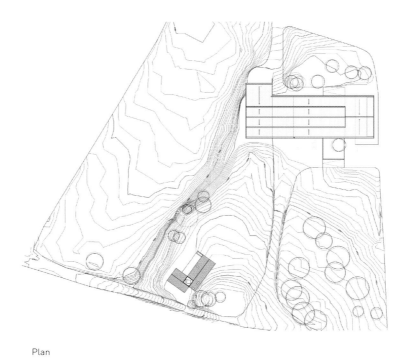

Plan

Herdade do Cebolal is a family run winery that was started in 1876 by Caio de Loureiro near the village of Vale das Éguas on the Costa Alentejana, at the southern end of the Península de Setúbal wine region of Portugal. The current owner, Luís Mota Capitão, runs the 200-acre organic estate, of which 50 acres are dedicated to vineyards and the rest are sheep meadows and forest. Situated between two mountain ranges and approximately 6 miles from the Atlantic Ocean, the estate is surrounded by historic cities, towns, and buildings that are all painted white. In fact, the name Herdade do Cebolal means "onion estate" in Portuguese, referencing the white vegetable. In 2013, the family opened its new 16,000-square-foot winery building, designed by the Portuguese firm, Ribeiro de Carvalho Arquitectos, from Azenhas do Mar further down the coast. The previous winery was a rudimentary structure, with a simple plan and pitched roof, an important reference point for the new project. Conceived as a "slight white object," that emerges prominently from the surrounding landscape, the new building is rectangular in plan with a shed roof at one end—above the visitor's center and tasting rooms—and a split gable above the production areas at the other. The industrial warehouse is oriented to the north, whereas the visitor's area faces south, with a large covered balcony on the upper level that provides views over the vineyards and distant landscape. Construction needed to be simple and quick, therefore a combination of a prefabricated concrete structure and steel truss roofing system was employed throughout. The exterior walls rest on concrete blocks and are made of isothermal sandwich panels (for optimal thermal performance) with a horizontal corrugated finish. A series of rectangular, square, and circular windows and openings provide a playful contrast to the simple volume of the structure. Similarly, while brilliantly white during the day, at night the building turns a light shade of blue, with the interior lighting signaling "something precious inside." Herdade do Cebolal is an agricultural project with a determined ecological philosophy, to be friendly to the environment and to seek global sustainability. All new winery buildings throughout the world should strive to achieve this simple and fundamental objective.

APPENDIX

ARCHITECTS' PROFILES

ABILLAMA, RAED is a Lebanese architect who received his Bachelor of Fine Arts degree in 1992 and Bachelor of Architecture from the Rhode Island School of Design in 1993. He later received his Master of Architectural Design from Columbia University, New York, in 1994. He then worked at Rafael Viñoly Architects PC from 1994 to 1996. There he was involved in and exposed to various large-scale projects. He established Raëd Abillama Architects in Lebanon in 1997. His vision was to create a studio that would include a wide array of professionals in both the design and production fields working side by side. To that end, he formed a parallel studio called A.C.I.D. (Abillama Chaya Industrial Design) that specializes in the production of architectural detailing and product design.

AGAG, ANA founded Anagag Ltd, a London based architectural studio in 2012, after having graduated from the Escuela Técnica Superior de Arquitectura in Madrid in 2006 and working for Foster + Partners in between. Anagag LTD works on small scale projects in the United Kingdom and Spain, focusing on residential, renovations, interior design, retail, and furniture design. For larger scale or public projects, the studio collaborates with the Borgos Pieper Architecture and Design Studio based in London and Barcelona. Ana Agag believes that the relationship between the architect and client is key to the right evolution of an architectural design. Creating a multidisciplinary team of professionals around the project will incorporate all design factors from the start and help achieve a unified and consistent work of architecture.

BALDAUF, HANS is a founding principal of BCV Architects in San Francisco. A Bay-Area native and a graduate of the Yale School of Architecture, he is an architect with a long-standing interest in the public realm. This interest has led him to pursue a wide variety of project types which at their core enliven the public realm, including mixed use urban projects, grand market halls and pro-jects as small as flower stands and bus shelters. Each design problem is considered both on its own terms as well as how it fits into the larger context. A LEED accredited professional, Hans is also a strong advocate of a wider vision of sustainability which incorporates inspiration from the tenets of the Slow Food Movement.

BEARD, RICHARD is a San Francisco architect and principal of Richard Beard Architects which he founded in 2014. With a father who was both a contractor and developer, and a grandfather who was a land planner, Richard was surrounded by architecture and design from an early age. The history of architecture particularly intrigued him: how it reflected various cultures and shaped public and private lives, feeling and emotion. Formerly with BAR Architects (Backen, Arrigoni and Ross) since 1980 and as a partner since 1991, Richard was elevated in 2010 to the College of Fellows of the American Institute of Architects in recognition of his contributions to the advancement of the practice of architecture. Richard Beard Architects was established to create a smaller studio environment specifically focused on residential design.

BELÉM LIMA, ANTÓNIO was born in Vila Real, Portugal, in 1951. He graduated in architecture from the Lisbon School of Fine Arts (ESBAL) in 1979. He has held several professional positions including Director of Architects at Pioledo Lda in Vila Real (1981-2005), and Director of Belém Lima Arquitectos in Vila Real since 2006. The firm Belém Lima Arquitectos is associated with the international engineering consulting company, Norvia, also based in Vila Real. In addition to his professional work, António Belém Lima has been a visiting professor at the Department of Architecture at the University of Minho (1999-2007) and at the Department of Architecture at the University School of Arts of Coimbra (since 1997). In 2003 he received the International Association of Art Critics (AICA) Architecture Award.

DE PORTZAMPARC, CHRISTIAN is a leading French architect and urban planner. Born in Casablanca in 1944, he graduated from the École Nationale Supérieure des Beaux Arts in Paris in 1970 and established his practice in the same city in 1980. Since then, he has been recognized for his bold designs and sensitivity to the environment, and his practice has expanded to New York and Rio de Janeiro. In 1994, he was awarded the Pritzker Prize in Architecture at the age of 50, the first French winner, and in 2004 he received the most prestigious city planning prize in France, The Grand Prix de l'Urbanisme.

FLATO, TED AND LAKE, DAVID Since co-founding Lake|Flato in 1984, Ted Flato has received acclaim both nationally and internationally for his artful and practical regional designs that leverage each unique site, incorporate indigenous building forms and materials, and respond to the context of their landscape. By employing sustainable strategies in a wide variety of building types and scales, Ted seeks to conserve energy and natural resources while creating healthy built environments. His recent focus has been on residential, higher education and eco-conservation projects, including the ASU Polytechnic Academic Campus in Mesa, AZ; the new Midtown Arts & Theater Center in Houston, TX; and the Naples Botanical Garden Visitor Center in Florida.

FREDRIK SVENSTEDT, CARL was born in Stockholm and grew up in Montreal. He holds degrees from Harvard University and the Yale School of Architecture and founded his Paris office in 2000. Carl Fredrik Svenstedt Architects experiment with a detailed-oriented process guaranteeing the creation of quality, sustainable buildings. The designs are based on material, "for architecture is about thinking, but also about making." Svenstedt's work, notably in solid stone construction, has been recognized internationally, and he has taught at numerous universities, including the Ecole Spéciale d'Architecture in Paris, the Confluence Institute in Lyon, and the Spitzer School of Architecture at the City University of New York.

GENTRY, JON AND O'CARROLL, AIMÉE founded Seattle based goCstudio in 2012. An internationally diverse background of experiences of the founding partners brings a creative approach to each project. The studio's work is driven by the unique opportunities and constraints of site specific projects which evolve through close relationships with clients, artists, and craftsmen. The architecture is strengthened through these relationships, grounded in a strong consideration of site, material, and craft resulting in authentic and tactile buildings. The completed works of goCstudio act as a partner to their community and site to create lasting human environments and experiences that enrich the cultural landscape. Aimée completed her studies at the University of Cambridge and the Architectural Association in London, whereas Jon studied at North Carolina State University where he earned his Master of Architecture degree.

GRACIA, JORGE is a Mexican architect who graduated from the Universidad Iberoamericana Noroeste in 1997. In 2004, he founded graciastudio with offices in Tijuana and San Diego. He is the recipient of multiple architecture awards and recognitions, both at the national and international level, including "30 promesas 2009" Grupo Expansion, "Design Vanguard 2012" *Architectural Record*, "Emerging Voices 2013" Architectural League of New York, "Obra del Año 2013" ArchDaily, "Best of the Best" Red Dot Awards 2014, and "10 Despachos generadores de cambio 201" Grupo Expansion Obras. He has lectured at Virginia Tech, the Australian Institute of Architects (2013), the Architectural Record Innovation Conference in Los Angeles (2014), and the Cooper Union in New York (2013). He is the founder of the Escuela Libre de Arquitectura (2014), in downtown Tijuana, where he is currently the Director.

HUGHES, THOMAS AND MORA, EUGENIA are a team of Argentinian architects based in the city of Mendoza, who design, direct, and manage architectural projects, seeking to achieve excellence in design and its successful execution, with a strong commitment to meeting the needs and expectations of their clients. The two graduated from the Facultad de Arquitectura y Urbanismo de la Universidad de Mendoza in 2000, and opened MH+A arquitectos in 2009. Their experience in real estate development projects of their own has given them an extensive knowledge of all the stages involved in the complex process of carrying out a project, allowing them to provide comprehensive advice to their clients to achieve successful results. Participation in public and private competitions has allowed them to form multidisciplinary teams capable of covering the most diverse topics and project scales, counting several awards and recognitions at both National and International levels.

KORTE, BRIAN's work champions the honesty of modernism with a commitment to practical yet artful solutions that marry the strength of ideas bonded to the landscape with a passion for authenticity, richness and well-crafted materials. After 17 years as a partner at Lake|Flato Architects in Austin, Texas, Brian ran his own boutique practice completing the construction at Epoch Winery and Tasting Room and Saxum Winery before joining Clayton Korte as Principal in 2016 to lead the firm's new San Antonio studio. With over 25 years of experience, he has designed award-winning residences, adaptive re-use, hospitality and other commercial projects in places across the country from California to Virginia.

MCCABE, MIKE is originally from Florida and graduated from the University of Tennessee at Knoxville in 1995 with a Bachelor of Architecture. Mike joined Walker Warner Architects in 1997 and has lived on the East and West Coasts of the United States, as well as in Poland, Germany and India. His time spent living overseas, as well as his travels within the U.S. have reinforced a deep appreciation for contextually appropriate design. For each project, Mike draws inspiration from the local cultural and physical context with a goal of combining the best principles of regional vernacular structures with a modernist point of view, resulting in timeless architecture that reflects the client's vision.

MUNAR, PAU AND MUNAR, RAFEL lead an architecture studio called Munarq that is based in Mallorca and focuses on the integration of architecture in the Mediterranean landscape. The firm specializes in local materials and traditional building techniques. Their study is based on offering quality service, always considering the site and landscape in their designs. They build houses, villas in the countryside, and renovations in Palma de Mallorca using natural materials, local stone, and sustainable environmental systems.

NADAU ET LAVERGNE is a French firm established in 2008 by Jérémy Nadau and Vincent Lavergne that is active in the fields of architecture, urban planning, industrial design, research, and the teaching of architecture. Both architects graduated from the École Nationale Supérieure d'Architecture de Paris La Villette. The practice consists of a diverse team of architects, town planners, landscape painters but also graphic designers, economists and scenographers. With studios in Paris and Bordeaux, Nadau and Lavergne lead project in France and several other countries.

POLAZZI, GIOVANNI; ANDREINI, LAURA; CASAMONTI, MARCO; AND FABI, SILVIA are the principals of Archea Associati with offices in Florence, Rome, and Milan. Giovanni Polazzi graduated in architecture from the University of Florence, and then obtained his PhD in architectural and urban planning from the same university. In 1988 he founded the firm Archea, conducting planning and research in the fields of architecture, town planning and industrial design. Laura Andreini graduated with honors in 1990 with a thesis entitled Project for the Realization of the Tokyo International Forum. During her studies and prior to graduation, Andreini began working in various architectural studios and founded Archea studio together with Marco Casamonti and Giovanni Polazzi. Marco Casamonti is a founding partner of the Archea firm, graduating with honors in 1990, winning a competition announced by the architecture faculty of Genoa the following year and receiving a study grant within the context of a PhD in architectural planning. Silvia Fabi graduated from the University of Florence, and then obtained a PhD in processes and methods of architectural planning at the University of Genoa. After a series of national and international competitions with the firms of Prof. Loris Macci and Prof. Aurelio Cortesi she began collaborating with the Archea firm in Florence in 1995, becoming a partner in 1999. She combines architectural research with criticism and theory on the subject, as well as pursuing a didactic career.

RAHOLA AGUADÉ, VICTOR graduated from the Escuela Técnica Superior de Arquitectura de Barcelona (ETSAB) in 1973. He worked with Jose Antonio Coderch before establishing his own practice, Víctor Rahola Arquitecte, in Barcelona in 1974. He taught at the Escuela Técnica Superior de Arquitectura de Barcelona from 1977 until 2010 and has been a visiting professor at several schools of architecture. In addition to his academic career, he has participated in several architectural competition juries, lectured extensively both in Spain and abroad, and continues to write regularly on architecture. From 2008 until 2015 Victor Rahola worked together with Jorge Vidal under Rahola Vidal Arquitectes.

RIBEIRO DE CARVALHO, JOÃO AND RIBEIRO DE CARVALHO, MIGUEL are architects based in the southwest coast of Portugal in the town of Azenhas do Mar. João Ribeiro de Carvalho graduated in Architecture from the Escola Superior de Belas Artes de Lisboa (ESBAL) in 1977, and Miguel Ribeiro de Carvalho studied Architecture at the Universidade Lusíada of Lisbon, the Politecnico di Milano, and graduated from the Universidade Autónoma of Lisbon in 2005. After several years working on their own and in collaboration with other offices the two established Ribeiro de Carvalho Arquitectos in 2007. The firm's reputation is based on a team structured to respond to all types of projects in the areas of architecture, urbanism, interiors, and design developed from conception to final construction stage. Both are members of the Portuguese Order of Architects.

TELLO ELORDI, GONZALO was born in 1974 and graduated in architecture from the Polytechnic University of Madrid. After 13 years of experience in design, project management, and construction management, he joined the global architecture and engineering group IDOM in 1999 and is currently Project Director of Architecture in Madrid. His work includes the development of new railway complexes such as the Intermodal Station of A Coruña, the High Speed Station of Tarragona, the North Station of San Sebastián, and the Atocha station in Madrid. He also has experience in unique public projects such as the Archaeological Museum of Córdoba, and private ones, such as the Bodega de González Byass, in Otero.

THOMPSON, KERSTIN is an Australian architect, born in Melbourne in 1965. She is the principal of Kerstin Thompson Architects (KTA), a Melbourne-based architecture, landscape, and urban design practice which she founded in 1994, with projects in Australia and New Zealand. She is also Professor of Design at the School of Architecture at the Victoria University of Wellington, New Zealand, and Adjunct Professor at the Royal Melbourne Institute of Technology and Monash University in Melbourne. Her work is extremely varied and ranges in scale and program, from art and design schools for universities to multi-residential developments, museums, police stations, primary schools, and commercial fit-outs.

VALSASSINA, FREDERICO was born in Lisbon in 1955 and graduated in Architecture from the Escola de Belas Artes de Lisboa in July 1979. He set up his own Lisbon studio in 1986, and since then has collaborated with other architectural studios, both nationally and internationally. He has undertaken many noteworthy rehabilitation projects, receiving the National Award for Urban Rehabilitation for his work in this area. The studio has also worked on projects in various fields and of different scales, such as the Herdade do Freixo Winery, in Alentejo, Alcântara's ETAR - wastewater treatment - in partnership with Manuel Aires Mateus and João Nunes, and the new Hospital CUF Tejo, in Lisbon, currently under construction. He holds the position of Guest Professor at the Faculty of Architecture at the Technical University of Lisbon teaching in the master's degree in Real Estate Development and has also presented his work in various international universities, conferences, and other events linked to architecture.

VIDAL, JORGE graduated in Architecture from the Escuela Técnica Superior de Arquitectura de Barcelona (ETSAB) in 2005. He also studied at the Academy of Architecture Mendrisio in Switzerland in 2004, and in the ateliers of Peter Zumthor and Valerio Olgiati. Furthermore, in 2003 he studied in Greece with Ellia Zenghelis thanks to a scholarship awarded to him by the Mies Van der Rohe Foundation. He is currently completing his PhD at ETSAB. Since 2008 he has been a professor of Studio Projects at ETSAB and was the director of a series of lectures known as Foros ESARQ, at the Universidad Internacional de Cataluña from 2010 until 2016. From 2008 until 2015 Jorge Vidal worked together with Victor Rahola under Rahola Vidal Arquitectes, and since 2015, he has been working privately through his own studio. He has been a guest lecturer in several schools of architecture throughout Spain and abroad, and also regularly writes about architecture.

VON ECKARTSBERG, CHRIS is a founding Design Principal of BCV Architecture + Interiors. A LEED Accredited Professional, Chris has a passion for hospitality projects that celebrate the intersection of food, wine, and sustainable lifestyle design. A graduate of Dartmouth College and the University of Pennsylvania, Chris enjoys design at all scales, from master planning, architecture, and interior design, to custom furnishings, and the sustainable food movement. His interest in Lifestyle/Food-related design has allowed BCV to form significant collaborations with leaders in the wine and food world to create projects that help build and sustain communities and culture.

WAECHTER, BEN founded Waechter Architecture (WA) in Portland, Oregon, to pursue architecture that heightens and informs the experience of community and landscape. Inspired by experiential and clear, distilled design, prior to forming WA, he worked locally and internationally with leaders in architecture including the world-renowned architect Renzo Piano (Genoa, Italy), and Allied Works Architecture (Portland, OR). Ben is an award-winning and published designer whose principles lie in providing bold forms arrived at through exercises in concept, distillation, and intelligent programming. His experience includes a wide range of building types, including cultural, hospitality, commercial, and multi- and single-family residential.

AUTHORS' PROFILES

RIERA OJEDA, OSCAR is an editor and designer based in the US, China, and Argentina. Born in 1966, in Buenos Aires, he moved to the United States in 1990. Since then he has published over two hundred books, assembling a remarkable body of work notable for its thoroughness of content, timeless character, and sophisticated and innovative craftsmanship. Oscar Riera Ojeda's books have been published by many prestigious publishing houses across the world, including Birkhäuser, Byggförlaget, The Monacelli Press, Gustavo Gili, Thames & Hudson, Rizzoli, Damiani, Page One, ORO editions, Whitney Library of Design, and Taschen. Oscar Riera Ojeda is also the creator of numerous architectural book series, including Ten Houses, Contemporary World Architects, The New American House and The New American Apartment, Architecture in Detail, and Single Building. His work has received many international awards, in-depth reviews, and citations. He is a regular contributor and consultant for several publications in the field.

DEUPI, VICTOR is a Lecturer at the University of Miami School of Architecture. His research focuses on the art and architecture of the Early Modern Ibero-American world, and mid-20th-century Cuba. His books include *Architectural Temperance: Spain and Rome, 1700-1759* (Routledge 2015), *Transformations in Classical Architecture: New Directions in Research and Practice* (Oscar Riera Ojeda Publishers, 2018), *Emilio Sanchez in New York and Latin America* (Routledge, 2020), and *Cuban Modernism: Mid-Century Architecture 1940-1970,* with Jean-Francois Lejeune (Birkhäuser Verlag, 2020). Dr. Deupi was also the President of the CINTAS Foundation dedicated to promoting Cuban art and culture from 2016-2018.

DEDICATION

To the memory of Carlos J. Deupi who loved wine and inspired everyone around him to appreciate it as well.
— Victor Deupi

BOOK CREDITS

Edited by Oscar Riera Ojeda & Victor Deupi
Introduction by Victor Deupi
Art direction by Oscar Riera Ojeda
Graphic Design by Julia Miceli Pitta and Lucía B. Bauzá

First published in the United States of America in 2021 by
RIZZOLI INTERNATIONAL PUBLICATIONS, INC.
300 Park Avenue South, New York, NY 10010
www.rizzoliusa.com

© 2021 Rizzoli International Publications, Inc. and Oscar Riera Ojeda and Victor Deupi

Publisher: Charles Miers
Editor: Douglas Curran
Production Manager: Kaija Markoe
Managing Editor: Lynn Scrabis

Front cover: Joseph Phelps Vineyards; photo by Bruce Damonte Photography (p. 250)
Back cover photos: Please see book interior for project and photo credits.

All rights reserved. No part of this publication may be reproduced, stored in a retrieval system, or transmitted in any form or by any means, electronic, mechanical, photocopying, recording, or otherwise, without prior consent of the publisher.

Printed and bound in Singapore

2021 2022 2023 2024 2025/ 10 9 8 7 6 5 4 3 2 1

ISBN-13: 978-08478-6958-9
Library of Congress Control Number: 2021931391

Visit us online:
Facebook.com/RizzoliNewYork
Twitter: @Rizzoli_Books
Instagram.com/RizzoliBooks
Pinterest.com/RizzoliBooks
Youtube.com/user/RizzoliNY
Issuu.com/Rizzoli